The B.A.S.T.A.R.D Method

A rebellious, no bs, roadmap to reset your life before it resets you!

Sarah Shard

Shard Publishing, Coaching & Consultancy

Book cover design: Sarah Shard, created using Canva Pro
Illustrations: Canva Pro

First Edition, 2025

ISBNs:
Paperback: 978-1-9192468-0-2
eBook: 978-1-9192468-1-9

THE B.A.S.T.A.R.D METHOD

The author of this book does not provide medical, therapeutic, or other professional healthcare services or advice. The information presented is of a general nature and is offered solely to support readers on their personal self-healing journey.

Results cannot be guaranteed. This book is intended for informational and entertainment purposes only, reflecting the author's personal experiences and perspectives on the topics discussed.

Any reference to experiences other than the author's own may be fictionalised and used only to illustrate a point. Where individuals are mentioned, names and identifying details have been changed to protect privacy. This work represents the author's personal views and life experiences and is not affiliated with, endorsed by, or reflective of any employer, past or present.

The author is not a licensed medical professional, and the contents of this book should not be considered medical advice. The practices and approaches described are intended as complementary to, not a replacement for, professional medical care.

Always seek the advice of your doctor or other qualified healthcare provider with any questions you may have regarding a medical condition or treatment, and before undertaking any new health regimen. Never disregard professional medical advice or delay seeking it because of something you have read in this book.

The author and publisher disclaim any liability arising directly or indirectly from the use or application of the material contained within this book.

Dear Mum and Dad,

Dad — thank you for always making me believe in myself. Your words became the backbone of this book and the mantra that carried me through the tough days.

Mum — my best friend, who loved me 5000. Everything good in me, everything strong in me, comes from you. I am the woman I am today because of you...

I know you're both watching over us from heaven, sat on the porch in your rocking chairs together and we will all continue to do all we can to ensure we continue to make you proud.

I L Y both 5000 and more,

Sarah x

Contents

Preface

I never set out to write a book. I set out to survive. And along the way, I found words, tools, and truths that stitched me back together when I felt broken beyond repair.

This isn't the polished, highlight-reel version of self-help. It's messy, raw, and rebellious. It's mine — and now it's yours.

The title might have made you laugh. Or flinch. Or wonder if you were allowed to buy a book with "bastards" on the cover. But that phrase has been with me for years. Every time life knocked me sideways — heartbreak, loss, disappointment — I would call or text my dad. And no matter how bad it was, he always signed off the same way:

"Don't let the bastards grind you down, love, Dad."

It wasn't just a throwaway line. It was a lifeline. His way of saying, "Get back up, even if you're shaking. Don't let them win."

When I lost him, those words took on a different weight. And then, losing my mum cracked me open in ways I couldn't have imagined. Death does that. It strips away the bullshit and leaves you staring at life as it really is fragile, fleeting, too short to waste on other people's expectations.

So, this book isn't just a project. It's a promise. To him. To her. To me. And now, to you.

It's for the person who's tired of pretending they're fine. The one who feels broken, lost, or like they failed at the life they were "supposed" to live. The one who scrolls through everyone else's curated happiness and wonders why they can't seem to find their own.

It's for the one who's ready to stop surviving and start living.

What you'll find in these pages isn't a buffet of theories or a 70,000-word doorstop of recycled advice. You'll find stories — some messy, some tender, some sharp enough to sting. There will be tools — short, practical, no-fluff. As well as interludes — Truth Bombs, Rule Breaker Moments, Permission Slips — because sometimes you need a jolt, sometimes you need permission, and sometimes you just need to laugh at the madness of it all.

This isn't random advice. It's a 7-part method I created, used myself, and will continue to teach to others.

This is not about perfection. It's about honesty. It's about dropping the mask, smashing the illusions, and finally deciding who the hell you are when nobody else is watching.

So, consider this your invitation. To read, to reflect, to rebel a little.

This is where we begin.

Introduction

Well done you. You got past this title, (which, let's be honest, scared a few people off) and opened the book. That tells me something important: you're ready.

You've had those moments where you stop and think: "What the f*** happened to my life?"

Maybe it was a heartbreak that floored you. A disappointment that stole your spark. A loss that left you reeling. Maybe it was none of those things — maybe it's just the quiet, nagging sense that you're living a life that doesn't quite fit.

And here's the truth: you don't have to stay stuck there.

Self awareness is the first step to real change.

What you'll find here is not theory for theory's sake. It's not a doorstop of a book padded with endless stories that don't sound like you. You don't need another buffet where you pick at a dozen half-useful tips.

You need the truth. The nuggets. The things that actually stick.

That's why this book is short, sharp, and unapologetically to the point. No fluff. No sugar-coating. No long-winded waffle that leaves you more drained than inspired.

Here's what you will find:

- Discover the illusions that are holding you back.
- Feel empowered to pause so you can finally breathe.
- Face and slay the critic that keeps you small.
- Reframe moments of pain but remember more of the good times.
- Figure out your values and boundaries that align with your truth.
- Rewrite the rules you've outgrown and figure out some new ones.
- Decide, once and for all, who the F you are.

By the time you turn the last page, you'll not only know what it takes to rebuild — you'll have the fire to actually follow through.

No waiting. No pretending. No excuses.

Because life is too short to be lived for someone else.

And the bastards?

They're not going to grind you down.

Not on my watch.

How to Use This Book

There are three ways you might find yourself reading this:

1. **The Curious Reader.** You love dipping into personal growth books to see how other people tick. You might not be at rock bottom right now, but you're curious, you want a spark, and you're always learning. If that's you, dip in, scribble in the margins, take what resonates and leave the rest.

2. **The Fed Up, Fired Up One**. You're sick of your own excuses. You're not broken but just disillusioned. You're tired of going through the motions, tired of "someday," and you're finally ready to do something different. If that's you, read this book straight through, do the exercises, and actually test them in your life. This is your corner-turning moment.

3. **The Healing Warrior.** You've been through deep trauma or grief and you're still finding your way. First — I see you. Second — this book might help you shift perspective, but it is not a replacement for therapy or professional support. If that's you — take what lands, skip what feels too much, and if old wounds open up, please work through them

with someone trained to guide you safely.

However, you've arrived here, know this: you're in the right place.

This isn't a book you have to follow like a rigid syllabus. You can pause, reread, reflect, skip ahead, or put it down and come back in a week. Some of the exercises will feel easy, others will stretch you — don't force it. Pick the ones that speak to you most and do them properly.

Most of all — be open. Be honest. Be willing to surprise yourself.

Because the method only works if you do.

Part One: Seeing Yourself in the Mirror

Before you can change anything, you have to see it clearly. This part of the journey is about recognising the bastards in your life, naming how they make you feel, and deciding whether you're ready to do the work.

Chapter One

Who are the bastards anyway?

Let's get this out of the way: the bastards are real.

They've been in my life, and I know they've been in yours.

As a lover of self-help books and a seasoned self-saboteur, part of me always suspected I'd one day be brave enough to write this book. Not just any book, but one written to help people like us. Not with theory, not with a PhD in psychology, not with a shiny "expert" label — but with real life.

So, who the hell gives me permission to do this?

Me.

The brave me. The me who has looked grief in the eye and come out fighting. The me who has felt broken by bastards of all shapes and sizes — the ones who sneak up when you least expect it, and the ones who slowly wear you down over weeks, months, even years.

The me who has broken her life apart and rebuilt it.

The me who has lost the people who meant the most to her and somehow kept breathing anyway.

And here's the thing: I'm still here.

And so are you.

The bastards did not win. The bastards will not win. Not if we stop feeding them.

The Bastards, Unmasked

We all face them —different names, different faces, but the same impact: they grind you down, make you doubt yourself, and leave you gasping for air.

Let me break them down:

1. The People Bastards

Bullies don't just exist on the playground. They grow up, the move in next door or they pretend to be friends whilst sending you passive-aggressive texts. They gossip at family dinners, and could even be stood at the school gates at pick up. Sometimes, they're even the people closest to you —partners, friends, relatives.

2. The Situation Bastards

Money or lack of it that has debt piling up. Bills that choke your joy. Jobs that drain the life out of you. Relationships that feel like cages. These aren't just circumstances —they're situations that quietly suffocate you until you can't tell where you end and they begin.

3. The Mind Bastards

And then, the loudest of all: the bastard in your head.

The voice that whispers: you're not good enough… who do you think you are… don't even try.

The little devil in your ear, the critic in the mirror. You can't escape it because it lives within you. And some days, it feels like it runs the entire show.

Why Call Them Bastards?

Because naming them strips their power.

Because swearing at them feels good.

Because "obstacles," "challenges," or "adversities" just doesn't cut it when something has left you gasping for air, doubting your worth, or questioning your right to happiness.

When I hear the phrase "Don't let the bastards grind you down," I don't just think of school bullies or online trolls. I think of anything or anyone that claws at your wellbeing, steals your spark, or convinces you to shrink.

That's what this book is about: helping you spot them, strip them of their power, and finally set the boundaries that let you live and breathe again.

A Quick Reality Check for You

Before we go any further, I want you to do something. Grab a pen, your phone notes app, or the back of a receipt if that's all you've got.

Make a note of the first three bastards that come to mind in your life right now. Do not overthink or question what comes to mind. We aren't looking for polite or pretty. Just name them.

It could be:

- A person.
- A job.
- A situation.
- A voice in your own head.

Now look at what you wrote. That's where we start. You will discover that once you name the bastards, you can face them. And once you face them, you can fight back.

The Rallying Cry

Here's my promise to you: the bastards don't get the last word.

Not the bullies, not the debt, not the toxic relationships, and sure as hell not the voice in your head.

This book is your armour, your battle cry, and your toolkit. By the end of our journey together, you won't just know how to survive the bastards — you'll know how to thrive because of them.

So, take a breath. Grip the book in your hands. And say it with me, out loud if you dare:

"The bastards will not grind me down. Not this time."

Chapter Two

How the bastards make you feel?

The thing about bastards — whether they're people, pressures, or that critic in your own head — is they don't just mess with your diary or your plans. They mess with your body. They creep into your chest, your breath, your sleep. They make your mind race and your muscles ache. They leave you tense, short-tempered, and snapping at people who don't deserve it.

They don't just drain your time. They drain you.

The Day I Broke

I'll never forget one moment in particular.

It was a couple of years after my dad died. From the outside, things looked great. I'd won an award at work, I was being recognised in my career, I looked like I had it together. But on the inside, I was running on fumes.

One afternoon, I was sitting at my desk when a colleague started telling me a funny anecdote. I should have laughed or at least smiled politely. Instead, something in me snapped. I went completely still, my chest locked, and the noise in my head finally went quiet— in the scariest way.

I must have given him some kind of death stare, because he froze mid-sentence, turned his chair, and just... stopped talking. I stood up slowly, desperate not to cause a scene, found a friendly face and asked if she could step outside with me.

The second we reached the hallway; she looked at me and gasped. "Sarah — what happened?"

And I broke. My chest collapsed, my throat tightened, and between sobs I heard myself say, "My dad died."

The grief, the stress, the exhaustion— it all came out at once. Even now, when I think about that moment, I can feel my airways tighten.

That's what the bastards do. They wear you down until the smallest trigger tips you into breaking. They make your body hold things you never meant to carry. They suffocate you quietly, until suddenly you can't breathe.

The Emotional Fallout

When the bastards show up in your life, the impact isn't subtle. It's not just "a bad day at work" or "a little stress at home." No. It seeps into your bones, hijacks your breath, and turns you into a version of yourself you barely recognise.

Maybe you've felt it:

- Exhaustion: the kind that sleep doesn't fix, because your mind never shuts up.

- Tightness in your chest: like you're bracing for impact, even when nothing's happening.

- Anxiety dressed up as productivity: rushing, over-committing, ticking boxes just to prove you're still in control.

- Anger: snapping at people you love, because you're carrying the weight of things you hate.

- Numbness: the scariest one of all. When you stop feeling altogether because it's easier than being crushed again.

This is what happens when the bastards grind you down: your body keeps the score.

The Quiet Cost

Not every breakdown is loud.

Sometimes the bastards don't come crashing in. They creep like damp in the walls. You don't notice at first, just a little discolouration, a faint smell. But by the time the wallpaper peels and the damp has settled in, they've already spread everywhere.

That's what happens when you let the bastards live rent-free in your head and your body. You don't see the damage right away. But quietly, they shrink your life until it's greyer, smaller, and harder than it ever needed to be.

Why Naming It Matters

Here's the thing: if you don't name the fallout, you normalise it. You convince yourself it's "just stress," "just being tired," "just how life is."

But once you call it what it is, you can't un-see it. Naming the bastards and acknowledging how they make you feel is the first step to loosening their grip.

Because awareness cracks the door open. And through that crack, light starts to pour in.

***

Quick Reflection: Where Are They Showing Up?

Take a moment before you move on.

- Where are you carrying tension right now — shoulders, jaw, chest?
- Who or what drains you the most?
- When was the last time you felt light?

Jot it down if you can. Don't overthink it. Let your gut speak.

This chapter isn't here to depress you. It's here to validate you. To say: yes, the fallout is real, and no, you don't have to live like this forever.

And listen closely: you are not broken, even if you feel that way. Feeling broken doesn't mean you are broken. It means you've been carrying more than one person should have to. And now it's time to put some of it down.

I remember the moment I froze after months of relentless bullying. Through tears and sobs I mumbled, "I think I'm broken, I can't do this anymore."

In hindsight, I wasn't broken. I had been pushed to breaking point. My body and mind simply stopped coping. I felt broken, but I was NEVER BROKEN! I just didn't know how to fight back, yet.

I am a different person now, stronger because of those bastards. (And yes, it feels good calling them that out loud!)

Now back to your journey. The next step, The Crossroads, is where change begins.

This can be your turning point.

Chapter Three

The Crossroads

Every journey has a turning point. That moment where you realise you can't keep going the way you've been going. You're standing still, staring down two paths: the one you know — safe, familiar, repetitive — and the one you don't.

That's the crossroads.

And here's the thing: no one else can stand there for you. No one else can make the choice.

How Do You Know You're There?

You know you're at the crossroads when life feels like it's happening to you, not with you. When you feel like a passenger on a train that's speeding somewhere you never bought a ticket for.

It might look like this:

- You're exhausted, not just tired.
- You feel out of control, like your days are run by other people's needs and expectations.
- You keep whispering to yourself, "something has to change," but you don't know what or how.
- You've tried numbing the feeling by keeping busy or maybe turning to food, drink, scrolling, shopping but the emptiness always creeps back.

That hollow, restless, suffocated feeling? That's the signpost. That's the crossroads.

My Crossroads

I had one long before I ended my relationship. I told him I'd had enough and that I needed a break. I moved out for a few months not because I was ready to end things, but because I needed to breathe. I needed space.

Those months were my crossroads.

And do you know what I did? I stood in the middle of the damn road for five months waiting to be rescued. I kept thinking someone would show up and tell me which way to go. That someone else would give me permission.

But no one came.

It finally hit me: if I didn't move, I'd stay stuck in that junction forever — paralysed by indecision, desperate for a saviour that wasn't coming.

The only person who could rescue me...was me.

The Brutal Questions

It was then I asked myself the two questions that changed everything:

1. If I looked at my future with him, was it the future I wanted?

What I saw was repetition. The same arguments. The same frustrations. The same flatness. Nothing was going to change unless I changed.

But the alternative? That was possibility.

- I could possibly be happier.

- I could possibly meet someone who could love me differently.

- I could possibly discover my dream home.

- I could become someone who felt successful.

Possibility felt risky, scary as f*** but it also gave me a glimmer of hope.

2. Would leaving hurt as much as losing my dad?

That was the kicker. Because nothing, and I mean nothing, would ever hurt as much as that. If I could survive the worst pain of my life, then surely, I could survive this.

That was the moment I realised I wasn't broken. I was standing at the crossroads, and I had to choose.

It might not feel as obvious to you and hopefully it doesn't because I would hate you to be feeling as broken and lost as I did. So, if you are unsure, let's think a bit differently.

The Train Test

Here's another way to picture it.

Imagine your life as a train. You got on years ago, maybe without thinking too much about where it was going. You sat down, got comfortable, settled into the routine of stops and starts.

But one day you look up and realise: this train isn't taking you anywhere you want to go. The view outside the window doesn't inspire you. The people sitting near you drain you. The destination on the board fills you with dread, not excitement.

Now comes the hard question: do you stay on that train because it's familiar or do you get up, walk down the aisle, and step off at the next stop?

Yes, stepping off is scary. It might mean waiting on a platform, not knowing exactly which train to take next. But it also means possibility. It means you're no longer speeding toward a life you don't want.

That's the crossroads in action.

What the Crossroads Really Is

It's not a place of weakness. It's a place of potential.

The crossroads doesn't mean you've failed. It means you're awake. You've stopped sleepwalking through your life, and now you see there are choices.

Yes, choosing hurts. Yes, it's terrifying. But staying stuck in the middle of the road or on the wrong train is worse. You'll get hit by every passing car. You'll keep going somewhere that isn't yours.

The only way out is forward.

Who Walks with You

Here's what I need you to know: you don't have to walk alone.

Sometimes, friends or family will walk a stretch with you. Sometimes it's a therapist, a coach, or even the words in a book like this one. And sometimes, yes, it's just you.

And that's okay. Because if you've got yourself, if you can learn to be your own best friend, in a way, you'll never really walk alone.

***

Quick Reflection: Your Crossroads

Right now, pause and ask yourself:

Am I ready to face my crossroads?

- If yes, what are the two paths in front of me? Which one feels like possibility, and which one feels like dread?

- If no, when was the last time I felt that sense of choice, of standing in the middle of a junction? And how did I know?

And if you were on the wrong train right now, would you stay on, or would you have the courage to step off?

Jot it down. Feel into it. Trust the answers that rise.

The crossroads is the line between survival and choice. Between drifting and deciding.

When you're ready, when you take that first brave step onto the path that's yours, everything shifts.

And that's where we're heading next.

If you've read this far, you already know you're standing at a crossroads.

Before we step forward, I want you to pause here with me.

Take a breath. Read the next section slowly.

Let it speak to the part of you that's ready for something more.

I Am an Evolution, Not a Revolution

You know what it feels like, don't you?

You have that dream of a bigger, better life.

You know there has to be something more.

You know this is not your purpose —this was never your destiny to be where you are.

It is a journey.

Sometimes we take the right road.

Other times we don't.

We get lost.

We have that vision for a life by design.

We can taste it, feel it, see it.

We know we are capable of so much more than we are allowing ourselves to give.

And yet, we get sucked back into the old ways.

Old reactions.

It feels like we're being pulled into a hole.

We take five steps back (sometimes more).

We let our old selves creep in.

The self that didn't believe in our potential.

The self that thinks change is scary.

It's okay.

We're protecting ourselves but we're also hurting our future selves.

It's okay to falter.

It's okay to feel frustrated and scared.

It's okay... even the best people on the planet let themselves down sometimes.

Be present.

Accept you have faltered.

Accept it's not perfect.

Then decide if you still want more.

Do you still want a better life?

Do you still want to feel freedom from whats held you back, kept you small?

Do you still want that fresh start?

Do you want to change?

Or do you want to stay right here in this moment?

The choice is yours.

The choice is ours.

The choice is mine.

I am an evolution, not a revolution.

Part Two: The B.A.S.T.A.R.D Method

If you've chosen to keep turning the page, you've chosen yourself. This is where the real work begins —seven shifts, seven tools, seven ways to take your power back.

Chapter Four

B is for Break

Break the Illusion

"You know this isn't about spiders?"

I froze. Of course it was about spiders. Or bugs in general. That was why I'd hired him, the hypnotherapist to help me stop panicking every time one scuttled across the room.

"It's just a thing you're focusing your anxiety on," he said, "because you don't want to face the reality."

Silence.

"No, it's about the bugs. Oh, and the neighbour is noisy when he walks up the stairs and it grates on me. Also, we sometimes get idiots who come to play football on the car park outside and that grates on me too. I need you to do your thing and hypnotise me, so I don't care."

He rolled his eyes but smiled. "Okay."

I stood up, drifted to the kitchen, and began rearranging cups and stacking pots, as if moving ceramics could shield me from whatever truth he believed I was avoiding.

"We'll leave it there for today," he said, "but when you're ready to be honest with yourself, we can pick back up."

*What the f***!*

Before I could say anything else, my partner wandered in, introduced himself to my "new friend," and they chatted about something — I don't know what. I'd switched off, still haunted by the accusation.

When my partner left the room, the therapist studied me for a moment. "Okay. I get it now."

Get what?

I still didn't get it.

"Do you give me permission to speak the truth? That's the only way I'm going to be able to help you."

He said it calmly, but in my head, I could see that famous scene from A Few Good Men about handling the truth. I didn't know if I could handle whatever observation he'd made, but I knew I needed help.

"Please, don't let me stop you."

"He's never going to change. You think things will get better. They won't. It's not about the spiders."

I froze. All of a sudden my never quiet mind was like a stuck record with the line "He's never going to change" on repeat.

He loves me, things will change. Won't they?

I didn't want to look at him because deep down I knew he was speaking the truth, but I was right, I couldn't handle the truth.

The problem wasn't in the corners of my apartment or under my bed. It was in the corners of my life and hidden in the deepest, darkest place in my mind — the place I never went.

I was fundamentally unhappy. Anxious. Trapped in a relationship, trapped in a life I never asked for. I didn't want to question it or look too closely in case it fell apart in my hands. So, I focused on the things I could control. Or thought I could. The irritating sound of a stupid soccer ball hitting against the building. The noise in the walls. The tiny black shapes darting across the floor. Because it was easier to believe my home was infested than to admit my life was.

That day was the first time I understood what it really meant to break the illusion. I had built an entire mental decoy system to protect myself from looking at the truth. It worked for a while. If I kept my focus on the bugs, the noise, the little things I could complain about or try to fix, I did not have to deal with the big thing. I did not have to face the truth which was the ultimate big thing I could not face.

Here's the thing, if you don't break the illusion, trying to keep the illusion up, well, that will eventually break you.

How to Spot This in Your Own Life

Avoidance rarely looks like avoidance. It hides under the surface of what feels like everyday life. You might tell yourself you're simply focusing on practical matters, but if you pause for a moment, you may realise you are keeping busy, so you don't have to face something that feels far more difficult.

Signs you might be doing it:

- You pour your time and energy into small, manageable problems while steering clear of anything that feels too big.

- You fill your days so completely there is no room for stillness or reflection.

- You react strongly to small inconveniences yet feel oddly flat about the big issues.

- You spend hours researching or planning ways to fix something that, in the grand scheme of things, is not all that important.

If you're not sure whether you're in avoidance mode, try asking yourself: If this small problem disappeared tomorrow, what would I have to face instead? If the answer makes you uncomfortable, you've found the crack in your mirror.

Avoidance is not weakness. It's often a way to cope when life feels too much. Sometimes it buys you time to gather the courage or strength you need. But staying there for too long keeps you in the same place, shuffling cups around in the kitchen while the real work waits in the next room.

For years, the story I was avoiding wasn't about spiders. It was about the life I thought I was building. I wanted the wedding, to be a wife, and to be a mother. My partner always said, "We will do all that." And I believed him. I clung to those words like a promise, a guarantee, a lifeline.

But it was ten years into our relationship. Ten years of "not yet" and "one day." Ten years of me convincing myself it was fine to wait, that this was just how our life was unfolding.

Then my dad died. And somewhere in the middle of that grief, something in me cracked open. When you lose someone who has always been your anchor, you start to see life differently. I realised I had been kidding myself. I was never going to have the wife-and-mother role with that partner. I had been living in an illusion because the truth felt unbearable.

Letting go of that illusion wasn't neat or graceful. It was ugly. It meant admitting that the picture-perfect life I had imagined — the one I thought I should have — wasn't coming. Not in the way I'd planned. It meant letting go not only of him but of the version of myself who believed she couldn't be happy without that role.

Was it really all his fault? Of course not. I could have faced reality sooner. I could have pushed for answers, given him ultimatums, or at the very least forced him to have the hard conversations. Instead, I blamed him.

Was I not a grown-ass adult? I had a job. I paid my bills. I had credit cards and could make my own decisions. On paper, I was responsible. But in many ways, I was still waiting for a husband to magically appear like prince charming in the fairy tales. If I'd found my person, (and I truly believed I had) why didn't the reality live up to my idealistic dream of happily ever after?

Because life isn't always as easy as the fairy tales make us believe.

Looking back, I can see that I spent years avoiding the mirror. Not the one in the bathroom, the mirror that shows your life for what it really is. I was scared of what I might see. I didn't want to notice the hairline cracks in the glass because once you see them, you can't unsee them. And when you can't unsee them, you have to do something about them.

Eventually, with the help of the therapist and through many tears, I did look. I held up the mirror and, for once, I didn't turn away. I saw the cracks. I saw the places where the truth had been trying to break through for years. And I saw the painful, ugly reality that the life I was living didn't match the one I had imagined.

And it made me sad.

I don't want you to wait as long as I did. Please don't spend years avoiding the mirror because you're afraid of what you'll find. Take time now to look for the cracks in your own reflection. It's not about tearing your life apart for the sake of it. It's about being brave enough to break the illusion and let go of the story that's keeping you stuck.

Letting Go of Perfection and the "Shoulds"

Breaking the illusion is not just about facing the truth you've been avoiding. It's also about letting go of the perfect picture you've been carrying around in your head. The "shoulds." The scripts you picked up somewhere along the way that told you how life was meant to look.

You know the ones:

I should be married by now.

I should have a baby by now.

I should be further along in my career.

I should be able to keep it all together.

"Should" is a trap. It makes you measure your life against an imaginary checklist you never actually agreed to but still feel like you're failing at. And perfection? That's the polished frame around the "shoulds" that makes the whole illusion look social media-ready while it quietly drains you.

The truth is a lot of those "shoulds" don't even belong to you. They came from family, culture, friends, films, and the kind of stories that tie worth to marriage, motherhood, or money. And when your life doesn't match that picture, you don't just feel disappointed. You feel defective. Like there's something wrong with you instead of something wrong with the picture.

We all have them. While writing this book, I went to a new hair salon. Halfway through my appointment, the stylist (who was 29) asked me if, when I hit my forties, I felt the same pressure she does now. She'd been told there was this list of achievements she should have ticked off by thirty, and she was overwhelmed by everything she hadn't done.

Letting go is not giving up. It's recognising that the life you thought you had to live is not the only one available to you. It's loosening your grip on the fantasy, so your hands are free to build something real. Something that fits who you are now, not who you were told to be.

When you release the "shoulds" and stop chasing perfection, you create space for truth. And truth is where real change begins.

Stop Delaying Happiness

Another big illusion I carried for years was this: when I lose weight, then I'll be happy.

Sounds familiar?

Here's the problem. The flip side of that thought was me telling myself I couldn't be happy at the weight I was. I tied joy, confidence, and worth to a number on a scale that kept moving around like a slippery little bastard.

And let me tell you, the day I dropped a dress size, the heavens didn't part, and angels didn't sing. I didn't suddenly wake up confident, glowing, and living my best life. I was just... me, in slightly smaller jeans, still carrying the same doubts and insecurities.

That's the catch with illusions: they dangle happiness like it's always on the next hook. The promotion, the ring, the house, the dress size. You get there and it's not enough, because it was never about the 'thing' in the first place. It's about the story you were telling yourself: I'll only deserve joy when...

But joy doesn't work on layaway. You don't earn the right to be happy later by beating yourself up now. You claim it in the body, job, or relationship you're in and then, if you want to change, you change from a place of worthiness, not desperation.

So, what illusions are you carrying around that make your happiness conditional? Let's drag them out into the light and test whether they actually deserve that much power over you.

That's what these next exercises are designed to do; drag those illusions into the light, strip them of their power, and expose the truth.

***

Exercises for Breaking the Illusion

1. The Spider Test

Think of the thing that is taking upmost of your mental space right now, the one you complain about, talk about, or think about the most. It might be work, a neighbour, your weight, a messy house, a friend who annoys you or maybe even bugs. These are your spiders.

Now ask yourself: If this problem vanished tomorrow, would you feel truly happy, or would you just find something else to moan about or focus on?

Your spider list is this list of things that even if resolved, you would feel that huge sense of relief.

When you hit the item in the list that makes you feel nervous or uncomfortable, pause and sit with this for a moment or two. Now turn to a fresh page and write it down, even if it feels uncomfortable or you want to cross it out straight away. That is the crack in your mirror. That's where your real work begins.

We can keep getting rid of the spiders but they will just keep coming. The cracks though, these are the scarier things to face. We can try to cover them with masking tape, but its still there, probably getting bigger.

Why it matters: When I finally admitted the problem wasn't spiders, I realised my real infestation was a life I didn't want to face. The sooner you name the truth, the sooner you can stop shuffling cups in the kitchen while your real life waits in the next room.

2. The "Should" Strip-Down

Write a list of every "should" that is sitting in your head right now.

- I should have...
- I should be...
- I should do...

Next to each one, write where that "should" came from. Was it your family? Society? A friend? A TV show? Your own younger self?

When you see the source, you can decide if it belongs to you now. If it doesn't, cross it out. Tear the page up if you need to. It's time to let that shitty "should" go.

Why it matters: "Should" is the most exhausting to-do list you never signed up for. Every one you cross off frees up space for something that actually belongs to you now.

3. The Rebellion Room

Exercise: The Rebellion Room

This is a mental space you can step into any time you need to face illusions head-on and smash them to pieces.

Imagine you have the key to a private room. Nobody else can enter. Nobody else will ever see inside. In that room, you can do whatever you need: shout, scream, argue, smash things. This is your rebellion space.

Now, here's the twist: today, we're going to fill that room with mirrors.

Each mirror represents an illusion you've been holding onto:

The perfect life you thought you *should* have.

The roles you believed would make you whole.

The lies you told yourself just to keep going.

Take a few minutes to picture them clearly. What does each mirror show you? Whose voice told you it had to be that way?

When you're ready — smash them. Smash every single one until there's nothing left but shards on the floor.

When you walk out of the Rebellion Room and lock the door behind you, you leave those broken illusions inside. You don't take them back with you.

This is your moment to say "Bye Bye Bastards".

Reflection:

As you leave, pause for a moment.

Ask yourself: *What truth do I want to carry out of this room?*

It could be something simple like:

- *"I don't need to live by other people's rules."*
- *"Perfection is not the goal."*
- *"My worth isn't defined by what I achieve or who I please." (This is my favourite)*

That truth becomes your anchor — a reminder that you don't need the illusions anymore. You've left them behind.

Why it matters: You can't rebuild your life on top of lies. I life built on a foundation of lies and shoulds is only going to become unstable and crumble. Smashing the mirrors is symbolic, but it tells your brain you're done carrying the weight of those illusions.

Breaking the illusion isn't about one dramatic decision. It's about catching yourself in the small ways you avoid the truth and then having the courage to look directly at it.

For me, it started with a conversation about spiders and ended with admitting my relationship was never going to give me the life I truly wanted, and, I'm going to say it – deserved!

Your version will be different, but the patterns are often the same. We fixate on the small problems, so we don't have to deal with the big ones. We clutch onto "shoulds" and picture-perfect plans because they make us feel safe. But safety built on a lie will eventually crumble.

You've looked at your avoidance. You've faced your "shitty shoulds." Now it's time to take it one step further.

Because when you've stopped chasing spiders, you'll be ready to start adjusting your mask.

***

Sometimes there are quotes and sayings that you grow up with, I have these. And dropped throughout the book you will find some that I think we need to rebel against! For this chapter, here are two I that stuck out:

"Good things come to those who wait."

Nope. Good things come to those who move. Waiting is just another form of stuck.

"You made your bed, now lie in it."

Beds can be unmade. Sheets can be changed. I'll make a new bed, thanks.

The Universe Has a Sense of Humour

You can fight it, you can avoid it, you can even outright say no — but sometimes life just laughs and shoves you exactly where you were meant to be anyway. My Dublin story is proof the universe doesn't always take no for an answer.

"Everything Happens for a Reason"

You've probably had someone throw this quote at you when your life is in bits: "Everything happens for a reason."

And if you've ever been in the thick of it — grieving, heartbroken, stressed out of your mind — you'll know it can feel less like comfort and more like a slap in the face. Because sometimes the "reason" is hard to see through the fog.

But every now and then, you get a story like this.

Many years ago, I applied for a promotion. At the time, I had personal stuff going on that had distracted me a little at work.

When I was offered the role, on a trial basis, I was torn. I wanted the job, but I knew in the back of my mind that the issues in my personal life could continue to distract me. Ultimately, I declined the role to protect my mental wellbeing and take the immediate pressure off.

And for a while, that decision haunted me.

Fast forward a couple of years. I was ready for a new challenge and handed in my notice. No new job. No plan. Just a burning need to figure out my next chapter.

Two weeks into my notice period, I was offered a new role in Dublin. All expenses paid. Apartment provided. The works.

I immediately packed my bags, and moved to a new city in a new country where I knew no one.

Second week in that role, I found myself sitting next to someone who told me that two years earlier, they'd applied for a job but got rejected. The person they offered it to had changed their mind, so they were second choice and took the role.

You guessed it. I was the person who'd changed my mind.

So regardless of whether I'd taken that first job or not, I'd have ended up in the exact same place, on the same team, doing the same job.

I was meant to move to Dublin. I'd rejected the first path, so the universe found another way to get me there.

Here's the thing: sometimes "everything happens for a reason" is just life's way of getting you where you need to be

— even if you take the long way round. And sometimes, it's not the universe, it's you. Deciding, walking away, trusting that the right thing will circle back if it's meant for you.

Either way, the reason doesn't have to make sense right now. It only has to keep you moving.

Chapter Five

A is for Adjust

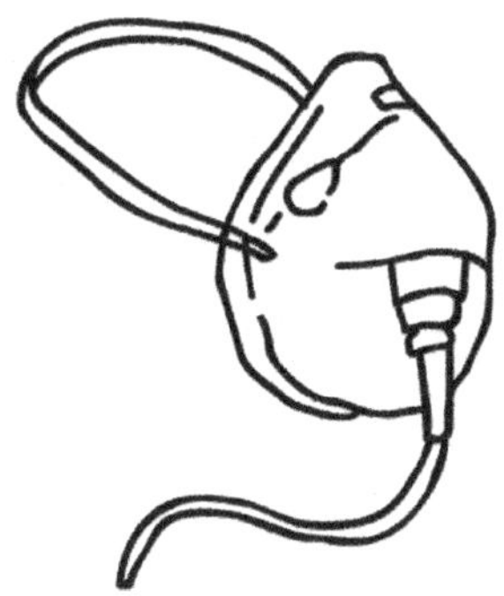

Adjust your Mask

I'll never forget that moment. I was sitting in the passenger seat of my auntie's car when another message came through from my mum, telling me how disappointed she was in me.

I froze. I couldn't speak. It was like I'd forgotten how to breathe. One tear slipped down my cheek, then another until there was no stopping it. The cries came in waves, and my whole body shook with each one.

My auntie reached across from the driver's seat and pulled me awkwardly towards her. My head rested on her shoulder while she stroked my hair. I felt like a little girl who had fallen over and couldn't make sense of the pain.

For context, my mum was an amazing mother. But in the last couple of years of her life, she developed mixed vascular dementia and Alzheimer's, and because I was the person closest to her, I often became the emotional punch bag. She could text me saying she loved me and then, sixty seconds later, tell me how disappointed she was, how disappointed my dad would have been, and that she'd never speak to me again.

As with anything in life, when we keep over-giving and putting everyone else's needs before our own, there will be a breaking point. Sometimes it's just one text or one more person asking you for something or one more moan from someone, and you just snap. It's never that "one" thing. More often, it's an accumulation of moments that leaves your chest tight and your oxygen supply running low.

The analogy of "put your oxygen mask on first" isn't new, but it's still relevant. I hope you never have those moments like I've had, when you feel overwhelmed, struggling to breathe, and unable to speak because you've given so much of your oxygen to others that you're left breathless, speechless, and empty.

Why Adjusting Your Mask Matters?

The mask I'm talking about here isn't a Halloween mask or a COVID mask. It's the performance mask — the one we put on, so the world thinks we're fine. The smile that says "I'm coping" when we're running on fumes. The "no worries" when we are quietly falling apart.

The trouble is, if you wear that mask for too long, it doesn't just hide what's going on inside. It starts to cut off your air supply. And if you've ever been on a plane and listened to the safety briefing, you know the rule: put your oxygen mask on first. Why? Because you can't help anyone else if you can't breathe yourself.

But in real life, many of us do the opposite. We run around making sure everyone else's mask is fitted properly while ours is hanging loose, barely keeping us alive. We give, and give, and give — until there's nothing left but resentment, exhaustion, and a body that's screaming at us to stop.

Another angle:

In your career, success can often be nothing more than a polished cover for exhaustion.

A couple of years after my dad passed, I won an award at work. Fancy London ceremony, the works. I smiled, posed for photos, and played the part.

A couple of months later — one of the peaks in my career — I was sat at my desk. A colleague was telling me some funny anecdote, and I just... stopped listening. From the way he trailed off mid-sentence and slowly turned his chair away, I can only assume I was giving him some level of death stare. The "if looks could kill" kind.

In that moment, all the noise in my head went quiet. My chest tightened. I couldn't breathe.

So as not to cause a scene, I stood up slowly, scanning the room for a friendly face. I found one. "Excuse me, can I chat to you for a minute?"

She followed me into the hallway. I turned to face her, and she just gasped, "Oh my God, Sarah — what happened?"

"My dad died."

And I broke. I sobbed beyond sobbing. I couldn't breathe. Even now, recounting that moment, I feel my airways closing.

That was over two years after his passing. Months of pushing, performing, and overdelivering — all while wearing the mask so well that even I believed it most of the time. Until my body decided it had had enough and ripped it right off.

Adjusting your mask means putting yourself back in the equation. It means realising that you can't show up as the partner, parent, friend, or colleague you want to be if you're gasping for air. It's not selfish. It's survival.

When you've been living in overdrive for years, it can feel unnatural to pause. You might even feel guilty for resting or saying no. But if you don't start now, your body will make the decision for you — through burnout, illness, or that moment when you find yourself in a car, unable to speak or breathe because you've given away all your oxygen.

How to Spot When You Need to Adjust Your Mask

When you've been running on empty for a long time, you can forget what "normal" even feels like. You start to believe that exhaustion, tension, and overwhelm are just part of life. But they're not. They're warning lights on your dashboard.

Signs your mask needs adjusting:

- You hold it together in public, then crash the second you're alone.
- You feel irritated or resentful when people ask for your help — even when you say yes.
- You can't remember the last time you did something purely because it brought you joy.
- You feel guilty when you rest, like you have to "earn" downtime.
- You find yourself daydreaming about running away or disappearing for awhile.
- You feel more like you're performing your life than actually living it.
- You get sick more often, or you're always "coming down with something."

If you're ticking several of these boxes, it's a clear sign you've been giving away too much oxygen. Adjusting your mask isn't about ignoring others — it's about making sure you're not running on fumes while trying to hold everyone else up.

***

Exercises for Adjusting your Mask

1. Permission to Breathe

Start small. Start with something as basic — and as essential — as breathing.

Right now, give yourself permission to stop. Instead of scrolling, answering emails, or mentally writing your to-do list, just be still. For 15 seconds, that's all.

Set a timer if you want to. Close your eyes. Feel your lungs fill with air as you breathe in. Feel them empty as you breathe out. Focus on nothing else but that rhythm.

When you're ready, build up to 30seconds, then to a minute. And then make it a habit: three times a day, set a reminder to stop and breathe. No multitasking, no distractions, just oxygen.

Why it matters: In my auntie's car, I had nothing left. If I'd been taking small moments to breathe and reset, I might have caught myself before I reached breaking point.

2. The Selfish Hour

When my mum had dementia, my mind was never my own. Was she eating? Was she safe? Had she washed? Every thought I had was wrapped around her welfare. And somewhere in the middle of that, I forgot that I was a person in my own right.

Yes, I was a daughter and a carer. I had a job. I was a sister, a niece, and a partner. But under all of those roles, I was still me. And me needed a break. Me needed to be selfish sometimes.

Being selfish in this context doesn't mean you stop caring about others. It means you care about yourself, too. You do something that brings you joy — or at the very least, a smile and a little peace. For me, sometimes it was as simple as watching reruns of Grey's Anatomy in my pyjamas. It wasn't productive. It didn't tick anything off a list. And that was the point.

Did I feel guilty? One hundred percent. Doing nothing and not being "productive" made me twitchy at first. I'd pick up my phone to text someone, then force myself to put it back down. It won't feel easy. And that's the point. Change is simple — no one said it was easy.

If you do feel guilt creeping in, pause and name two or three things you've already done for others that day. Remind yourself you've earned the right to balance. You need to breathe too.

Why it matters: If you never prioritise yourself, you end up like I did; out of oxygen, out of composure, and out of time.

3. The Oxygen Leak Audit

If you've ever had a slow puncture in your car tyre, you'll know how sneaky it is. You don't notice it at first, just a little pressure gone here and there until suddenly, you're riding on the rim. That's what happens when you keep giving out your oxygen without realising where it's going.

This exercise is about finding your leaks.

For one week, keep a simple log of where your time and energy go. Every couple of hours, jot down what you've been doing and how it made you feel:

- Did it energise you?
- Did it drain you?
- Was it neutral?

By the end of the week, you'll start to see patterns. Maybe your mornings are swallowed by other people's emergencies. Maybe certain people leave you flat every time you speak to them. Maybe you spend two hours a day on social media and feel rubbish afterwards.

Your job is to plug at least one leak. That could mean setting a boundary, saying no, cutting something back, or delegating. Even one plugged leak can give you more oxygen than you realise.

Why it matters: You can't keep refilling your oxygen if it's constantly leaking out somewhere else. Plugging even one slow puncture can give you more capacity than you think.

Adjusting your mask means reclaiming your air supply before you pass out from giving it all away.

For me, it took that moment in my auntie's car, struggling to breathe and unable to speak, to realise I couldn't keep going like that. I had been so focused on keeping everyone else safe, fed, and happy that I'd starved myself of the very things I needed to survive.

Now it's your turn to notice:

- Start with your breath. Give yourself permission to stop, even for 15 seconds.

- Take a selfish hour. No guilt, no explanations.

- Find and plug your oxygen leaks.

It won't always feel easy. If you've spent years ignoring your own needs, it will feel awkward, rebellious, and maybe even wrong at first. But those are just the side effects of change.

The more oxygen you give yourself, the stronger you'll be for what comes next. Because now that you're breathing again, it's time to face the voice that's been living rent-free in your head for years — the one that tells you you're not enough, you're behind, or you're not allowed to want more.

In the next chapter, we're going to meet your inner critic. And then, we're going to slay the bastard.

***

"Keep your head down and work hard."

I kept my head down so long I forgot what the sky looked like. Now I work smart and keep my head up.

Rule Breaker Moment

D.I.L.L.I.G.A.F.

I remember the day my dad discovered this word. DILLIGAF.

He called me from his holiday, laughing down the phone. He'd gone into a shop and there was a customer chatting to the guy behind the counter reeling off some boring story that he'd probably heard a thousand times.

Somewhere along the way, when the customer finally left, the guy turned to my dad and said that when he had customers like that, he sometimes just wanted to say: DILLIGAF.

That was the first time my dad heard it. If you've never come across it before, it stands for: Do I Look Like I Give A F***.

He loved that word. He thought it was brilliant —and he kept dropping it into conversations afterwards, usually with a cheeky grin.

And I'm dropping it here for you too. You don't have to say it out loud, but maybe in those moments when you know deep down you don't need to care, it can give you a little nudge. A little smile.

Because here's the truth: the less you care about the things that don't serve you, the more energy you have for the ones that do.

So next time something drains you, ask yourself one thing:

DILLIGAF?

If the answer's no... walk away smiling.

Chapter Six

S is for Slay

Slay your Inner Critic

"Sticks and stones may break my bones, but words can never hurt me." Who else was told this as a child by parents who were trying to protect us from bullies?

Here's what you learn as an adult: bones mend and cuts heal, but words — those sneaky little f***ers — can cut deep and haunt you for years. And if you're anything like me, the bullies don't hold the monopoly on hurtful words.

No one — no person, no group — has ever hurt me as much as my own inner critic. That voice in my head? She's relentless.

You wanna call me fat? Okay. I own a mirror.

You wanna tell me I'm not good enough? Guess what — I've probably told myself that five times since breakfast.

You think I'm too confident? That I act like I know it all? So what? I'm probably only showing half the confidence I actually have and sharing half my knowledge, just so I don't make other people uncomfortable.

But who feels uncomfortable in the end? Us. Always us. Because we can be our own worst enemy.

No words can hurt me as much as the ones I use to hurt myself — courtesy of my doubter, my inner critic, my internal bastards.

And here's the interesting bit: there's a theory that your inner critic's voice is one you recognise. Maybe it's a parent, a sibling, a teacher, an ex. Somewhere in your subconscious, you stored the things they said — the digs, the warnings, the "helpful advice" that kept you small — and now that voice is yours. It sticks.

The way I see it, when your inner critic is in overdrive, it's running on either stress or fear.

In my years as a carer for my mum, the critic fed off stress: I'm not being a good enough daughter.

Other times, it's pure fear: fear of failure, fear of success, fear of not being enough, fear of being alone.

Like the first December after I split with my ex and moved into a luxury apartment block.

When I signed that lease, I was buying into a vision of who I wanted to become; the confident, outgoing, bubbly Sarah — not the anxious, quiet, introverted woman I'd been for far too long. This place cost more than double my old rent, and in my head, it came with a new personality.

So, when I got a text inviting me to my neighbour's apartment for festive drinks and nibbles, I was ready. I bought expensive wine. I picked out a sparkly Christmas jumper — classy, I told myself, though let's be honest, "classy" is relative when there's a glitter reindeer on your chest. Still, it felt like the perfect mix of fun and festive.

I even found ways to drop it into conversation with friends: I'm off to a Christmas gathering with the neighbours. It made me feel like I belonged there already.

The party started at 7pm. I told myself I'd be fashionably late.

Music started. Laughter drifted through the walls.

Just a little longer.

8:00pm — What if no one talks to me?

8:30pm — I don't know everyone's names. What if I blank and can't remember?

9:00pm — What if I have nothing intelligent to say? I'll look like an idiot.

9:30pm — Oh shit, now I'm going to look rude for being this late. What excuse can I give? They can see my lights are on. Shit.

I don't think I need to tell you how this ends.

It was just festive drinks. They were just people. We already had something in common — we lived in the same building, and we all celebrated Christmas. Those two topics alone could have started a dozen conversations.

But that voice in my head had been busy all night, feeding me questions that all came from the same root: I'm a fraud. I'm not the confident, bubbly neighbour I imagined. They'll see I'm not good enough to live here. I'm not interesting enough on my own to be accepted by new people.

Sound familiar? Maybe not the bailing on mince pies and Buck's Fizz, but the part where you don't go, or you hold yourself back, because the voice in your head says you're not good enough.

Meet Your Inner Bastard

That night in my apartment, I wasn't being logical. I was being hijacked. And that's what your inner critic does — it hijacks your thoughts, plants doubts and convinces you they're facts.

It's sneaky because it sounds like you. It uses your voice, your memories, and your deepest insecurities as ammunition. It doesn't just whisper "don't go" — it spins you a whole believable story about why you shouldn't. And when you've got no oxygen in your system (remember Adjust Your Mask?) and you're already running on stress or fear, it's even louder.

Most of the time, your critic has two main fuel sources:

- Stress-fuelled: when you're overloaded, exhausted, and doubting you can cope. (I'm not a good enough daughter, friend, boss, partner.)

- Fear-fuelled: when you're stepping into something new or vulnerable, and your brain wants to keep you "safe" by keeping you small. (I'm not ready. I'll mess it up. I'm not like them.)

The irony? Your critic thinks it's protecting you. That voice believes it's saving you from embarrassment, rejection, failure, or hurt. It doesn't realise that by keeping you "safe" inside your comfort zone, it's actually suffocating you.

When you're under its spell, you might not even notice. The thoughts just feel true. You think you're being "realistic" or "sensible" when actually, you're obeying a voice that's been living rent-free in your head for years.

And remember: that voice often isn't originally yours. It's borrowed. Somewhere along the way, you absorbed someone else's opinion, criticism, or expectation and your brain filed it under "truth." A parent, a teacher, a sibling, an ex — anyone whose words once carried enough weight to stick.

Recognising that voice for what it is — not fact, just fear — is the first step to slaying the bastard.

Spotting the Bastard in Action

Your inner critic is good at disguise. It doesn't announce itself with "Hi, I'm here to ruin your confidence." It slips into your thoughts like it's doing you a favour. But there are ways to catch it in the act.

Here's how you know it's the bastard talking:

- It uses absolutes: "You always mess up." "You never get it right."
- It predicts the future like it's a fact: "This will be a disaster."
- It compares you to others and makes sure you lose.
- It drags up your greatest hits of shame at the worst possible moments.
- It poses as "common sense" but leaves you feeling smaller, not stronger.
- It repeats phrases you've heard from someone else in your past.

The moment you spot it; you've got a choice. You can let it keep driving, or you can pull it over and ask some questions.

Fact or Fiction?

When you catch the bastard in action, ask yourself one simple question: Is this real?

Is it a fact I can prove? Or is it a story I've been telling myself?

Facts can be backed up with evidence: "It's raining" (look outside). "I missed that deadline" (check the date).

Fiction is built on assumptions, guesses, and fear: "They won't like me." "I'm not good enough." "I'll make a fool of myself."

Once you start separating fact from fiction, you see how much of what's been holding you back is just a badly written plot line you've been reciting on autopilot.

My Fiction Became Fact

A few years ago, my inner critic almost stopped me from doing something that changed my life. I'd started writing fiction as a way to distract myself from my own thoughts a little creative escape. I had no training, no degree in creative writing, no "right" to call myself an author. Just me, a busy brain, and a notebook.

The more I wrote, the more the bastard voice piped up. Who do you think you are? No one will ever read this. You're wasting your time. So, I kept it all to myself.

Until one day, I saw a national competition run by a top publisher. On a whim and against every protest from that inner critic, I submitted a pitch and the first few chapters of one of my novels.

And I was shortlisted.

First time letting anyone read my work. No credentials. No special training. Just me, finally deciding not to believe the fiction in my head and seeing what would happen if I acted anyway.

That's the thing about slaying the bastard. You don't have to silence it completely you just have to stop letting it be the author of your story.

And now it is time for you to face your inner critic or your villain, whatever you choose to call it. Lets face it together.

***

Exercises for Slaying your Inner Critic

1.Cast Your Villain

Your inner critic isn't just a voice, it's the villain in your story. And like any good villain, it's got motives, weaknesses, and a role to play.

Think about your favourite films or books. Most of them end when the villain is defeated, silenced, or outsmarted. The hero wins not by pretending the villain isn't there, but by knowing their moves and refusing to be ruled by them.

Your job is to cast your inner critic as that villain. Give it a name, a face, a voice. Make it vivid. The pettier and more over-the-top, the better, the more you can separate it from you.

Once you've got your villain, you can start treating every interaction with it like part of the plot. Your mission isn't to let it narrate your life. Your mission is to make sure your story ends with the hero — you — standing tall while the villain fades to nothing.

2. The Bastard's Greatest Hits

Grab a piece of paper and write down the top five lines your critic throws at you. The ones that make you hesitate, hide, or hold back.

Now, for each one, write a comeback in your strongest, most unapologetic voice. You don't have to be polite — this is your private list.

Example:

Critic: "You're not good enough."

You: "Good enough for who? And why the hell do I care?"

Keep this list somewhere you can grab it when the bastard pipes up.

3. Fact or Fiction Filter

Next time the critic says something, pause and run it through this filter:

1. Is this a proven fact I can back up with evidence?
2. Or is it an assumption, prediction, or old story I've been carrying?

If it's fiction, rewrite it on the spot into a fact you'd like to be true. Example:

Critic: "You'll embarrass yourself."

Rewrite: "I might feel nervous, but I'm capable and prepared."

The more you practise this, the more you'll catch the bastard in the act and the less power it will have over you.

Slaying the bastard doesn't mean you'll never hear that voice again. It's been with you for years, and it's not going to pack its bags overnight. But it does mean you stop giving it the microphone.

That night I stayed in my apartment instead of walking across the hall, the critic won. It ran the whole show, fuelled by fear, until I believed every word it said. But the day I hit "send" on my novel pitch, it lost. The facts didn't change — I still had no degree in creative writing, no formal training, no reason to expect I'd be taken seriously. The only thing that changed was I stopped obeying the fiction in my head and tested it against reality.

And reality proved the bastard wrong. I was shortlisted by a top publisher the very first time I let anyone read my work.

This is your proof that the critic isn't a truth-teller. It's just a villain in your story, and like all good villains, it can be defeated. You don't have to silence it completely to win, you just have to keep showing up, keep testing its lies, and keep writing your own plot.

The more you challenge it, the weaker it gets. The more you act in spite of it, the smaller it becomes. And one day, you'll realise it's not running the show anymore — YOU ARE.

So, sharpen your sword, hero. The bastard might still mutter in the corner, but you've got a story to live, and it doesn't get to write the ending.

"Stop showing off."

What if showing off is just showing up? I'm not dimming myself to make others comfortable.

This one is one of the biggest for me to overcome. I recall my mum and grandmother saying this to me from an early age and even this last year. Whenever I would mention being good at something or an achievement, it was often the same reply:

"Self praise is no recommendation."

If I don't praise myself, who will? Self-praise is self-recognition — and I'll recommend myself all day long.

Permission Slip: Grief is the Price We Pay for Love

The first time I read this line, I felt it. The kind of quote that stops you in your tracks.

If the price you pay for loving so deeply is grieving so deeply, would it stop you from loving that way?

You might answer differently than I would. I think about how my mum would answer. She grieved my dad for over ten years. Every single day. It changed her; in some ways good, in other ways painfully sad.

Would she have chosen not to love him if she'd known the depth of her grief? Not a chance. They adored each other for forty years, eyes only for one another. Her sorrow was fierce because her love was fierce. The tears she cried matched the love they shared.

When my dad died unexpectedly, it felt like my world had shattered. Grief wasn't just emotional; it was physical, like a knife twisting constantly. If you've felt it, you know. If you haven't, you can't truly imagine it.

But here's the thing: I loved my parents deeply. And if my grief is simply the shadow cast by that love, then so be it.

Because death isn't the only thing we grieve. And that's what I want to point out here.

In Chapter Three, I talked about being at the crossroads and deciding to change trains. Well, being brave enough to change direction; to leave a relationship, to quit a job, to let go of a dream comes with its own kind of grief.

My mum grieved my dad, but she also grieved the retirement years she thought they'd share.

When I ended my relationship, both me and my ex grieved for the future we had once promised each other.

Even in work, you might start a job full of hope, convinced it's the best move of your life. Six months later, you're drained, stuck in another toxic environment. You grieve the vision you once had of that role.

Grief isn't just about death. It's about lost futures, abandoned dreams, and versions of life we thought were guaranteed.

And that grief? It's proof of how much we cared.

Here's the reframe I want to leave you with grief is not weakness, it's evidence. Evidence that you dared to love, to hope, to risk, to imagine. Evidence that you lived fully, not half-heartedly.

So yes, grief is the price we pay for love. But what a privilege it is to have loved and to have cared that much at all.

Grief is proof that love mattered. You don't need to rush through it or make it palatable for other people; this is your space to feel it all.

Chapter Seven

T is for Time Traveller

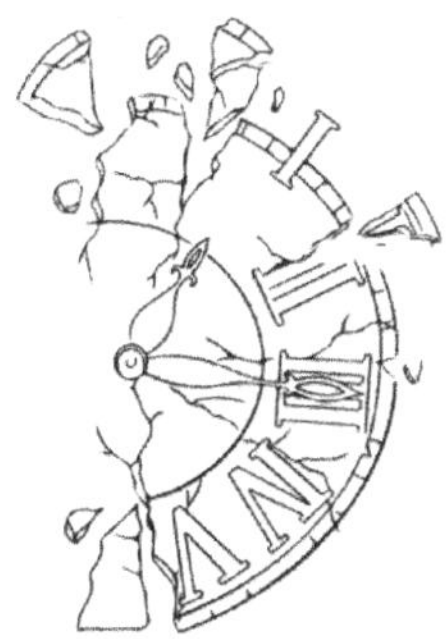

Talk to your Time Traveller

At this point in many self-help journeys, you'll be pointed back to your childhood and told to heal your "inner child." I'm not dismissing that at all. I have done my fair share of therapy around inner child healing and facing the younger red haired Sarah of my childhood but that never really resonated with me which resulted in a lack of real results or realisations. As I say, not dismissing it, for many people, it works and that is great, for them.

I'm an adult. My childhood experiences shaped me, sure, but they don't define everything I've become. So instead of asking you to cradle your inner six-year-old, I want you to try something different: time travel.

Humour me here.

Not the kind with a flux capacitor (80s movie reference, tick). If I could time travel for real, I probably wouldn't be sat here writing this book. I'd be off living a dozen different "best lives." But time travel as I see it is about revisiting your own memories, giving them space, and deliberately choosing how you carry them forward.

Because here's the truth: the past isn't something you just "get over." It's something you carry. Sometimes lightly, like a stone in your pocket. Sometimes so heavy it feels like a boulder on your back. And when your brain replays the hard stuff on loop, the joy can often get buried under it.

Time travelling is my way of interrupting that pattern. You can't delete the hard moments, but you can rebalance them. You can train yourself to remember joy as strongly as you remember pain.

My Memory Quilt

I love those American shows where generations of a family sit together and quilt — each square telling its own story. Tradition, memory, and love all sewn together.

Now, this isn't Quilting with Sarah, I leave the real crafting to others, but I do want you to use your imagination here to imagine your own quilt: a double-sided quilt of memories.

On the front side, every square holds a positive memory. For me, I'd stitch in:

- My dad pulling his trousers up to his chest just to make us laugh.
- Him telling stories from his day while we ate dinner.
- All of us sat around the table each evening, because we weren't a TV dinner family.
- The sound of my mum saying "Yes" when she finished a Wordsearch.
- The feeling of my mum's hugs and — if I'm honest — I'd give anything for her to make me a sandwich

again.

Those memories make me feel warm, safe, and grounded like being wrapped up in love.

On the back side, the quilt looks very different. Here I'd stitch in:

- Falling out of the car when I was about four or five — my second earliest memory.
- The day a girl at school threatened me when I was ten.
- My first funeral. And the many others that left me shaken.
- And, in more recent years, the two worst days, losing my parents.

These squares don't feel cosy. They sting. But they're still part of my quilt and they all helped shape me, in very different ways.

My Own Quilt Squares

To give you an idea of how this can look, let me share two squares from my own quilt.

On the happy side, one of my clearest memories is the sound of my dad's laughter. I remember one time he re-told, in his usual comedic style, a story from his day. It was something about a man with a wig who thought no one knew it was a wig — so everyone played along and acted shocked when he finally told them. My dad laughed out loud telling that story, and we all laughed with him. He had on an orange t-shirt, he was sat on the sofa in their apartment and we were together with other members of the family for a birthday. That moment is engraved in my memory, and even now, when it flashes through my mind, it makes me smile instantly.

On the painful side, I'll never forget the moment I walked into the family room at A&E. My mum just shook her head, tears falling, and whispered: "He's gone." That memory is tattooed on my heart forever.

But here's the shift. When I think of that painful square, I try to bring the laughter square to mind straight after. The wig story. My dad's laugh. His joy. It doesn't erase the grief, but it softens it. It pulls me from frown to smile. And I know — deep down — that's what he would want for me.

Exercises for Talk to your Time Traveller

1.Sketch Your Quilt

Grab two blank pages. On one, draw a simple patchwork grid for your positive memories. On the other, draw a matching grid for the harder ones. No art skills required, stick figures and single words are perfect. The point is to give your memories a home outside of your head.

Fill in the Squares

On the front page, jot down the memories that make you smile, laugh, or feel warm. On the back, note the ones that still hurt.

Pick Three "Back Squares"

Circle three of the hardest memories and three of your happiest. For each hardest memory:

Spend 15 seconds thinking about it. Really let yourself feel the sting.

Then flip to the front. Pick one happy square and spend 45 seconds replaying it in detail. The sights, the sounds, the emotions.

Why it matters*:* This is about helping you to rewire your brain to remember the happiness more than the sadness. It takes time, but anchoring in these memory flips can help you to rewrite them.

2. Wrap Yourself in It

When you're done, imagine your quilt sewn together, front and back.

Now, take it one step further. Take another moment to look at both sides of quilt and then sitting comfortably and ideally in a quiet place, close your eyes. (I suggest reading this section before closing your eyes, otherwise you won't know what to do.)

Picture yourself wrapping it tightly around your shoulders. Feel the weight of it, heavy enough to comfort you, but not so heavy it drags you down. Let the softness of those joy-filled squares rest against your skin.

Notice what happens to your breath when you do this. It slows. Your shoulders drop. Your chest loosens. That's the power of giving your nervous system a physical symbol of safety and love.

Even if the painful squares are stitched in on the other side, they don't have to be the part that touches you every day. You get to choose which side you face inward. You get to decide which memories live closest to your heart.

The Gratitude Lens

Here's the other piece of time travelling: gratitude.

It might feel strange to even think about being grateful for the moments that hurt you. For the bullies, the heartbreaks, the losses. But without them, you wouldn't be exactly who you are today.

I'm not asking you to thank the people who caused the pain they don't deserve that. What I *am* asking is that you consider thanking yourself. For surviving. For carrying on. For learning lessons you couldn't have learned any other way.

Every scar tells you something. Every heartbreak cracks you open to a deeper capacity for love. Every rejection pushes you closer to where you're meant to be. You might not understand it in the moment, but you can accept that right now, you are standing exactly where you need to be.

3.Quick Reflection

Think of one painful square on your quilt.

Ask yourself: *What did this moment teach me? What strength did I discover because of it?*

Write a gratitude statement for it.

"That breakup showed me I deserve more than a life filled with empty promises."

"That bully made me stronger in standing my ground and knowing where I should lay boundaries."

"That loss reminded me how precious love really is."

Gratitude doesn't erase the pain, but it reframes it. It turns "why me?" into "look at me now."

Anchoring the Reset

Here's the best part: once you build your quilt, you'll see you have far more joy squares than you thought. They were just buried. And you'll realise you can choose which side to carry against your skin.

That's the essence of time travelling: you're not denying your past, but you're deliberately choosing how to carry it forward.

And remember: your quilt isn't finished yet. There are blank squares waiting for moments you haven't lived yet. Future laughter. Future love. Future adventures.

What do you want those new squares to hold? The sound of your own laughter echoing louder than your doubts? The day you finally said yes to something bold. The moment you realised you were living the life you once only dreamed about.

Every choice you make from here is another square stitched in. And the best part? You hold the needle now.

This is not a once and done, it's a tool for you to revisit as often as you like, and you can also think of other ways to rethink those memories you wish you could change.

So, if Chapter 6 was about silencing your critic, this chapter is about grounding yourself in the truth that your past does not get to define your future. It's part of the fabric of who you are — but you choose how to wear it.

And that choice will give you the strength you need for what comes next: Aligning with Your Truth.

***

"Children should be seen and not heard."

That's how you raise people who silence themselves as adults. I've found my voice now — and I intend to use it.

Truth Bomb

Goodbyes aren't always clean cut. Sometimes they drag, ache, and unravel over weeks, months, or years and in that stretch, you learn who you really are.

The Long Goodbye

With dementia, you don't lose someone all at once. You lose them piece by piece.

There were so many moments when I'd notice a little part of my mum slipping away; her memory, her independence, her spark. We'd already said a hundred small goodbyes before the day finally came to say the last one.

I never knew the last gift she ordered me on Amazon would be the last gift. I never knew the birthday before she died would be the final one where she insisted on "buying me something," even though I chose it and wrapped it myself.

Her death was sudden, heart-breaking, and final. But the truth is, we'd already been grieving for years. That's the cruelness of the long goodbye; you're losing someone even while they're still right there with you.

But here's the other truth: it teaches you things.

It teaches you that holding on too tightly can sometimes hurt more than letting go.

It teaches you that love is not about clinging, but about being present in the moments you do have.

And it teaches you that life is far too precious to be lived half-heartedly.

The long goodbye showed me the importance of living passionately, of not waiting for "one day." Because sometimes, one day never comes.

And this is where the brightness sneaks back in. Because when you've lived through a long goodbye, you don't just carry the pain — you carry the clarity. You see, with fresh eyes, how short life really is. You stop putting off the trip, writing the book, taking the risk.

You laugh louder, love harder, and breathe deeper because you know how fragile it all is.

So, if you're walking through your own long goodbye; with a person, a relationship, a dream, or even with the version of yourself you used to be, let it teach you. Let it strip away the bullshit. Let it push you into living more fully, not less.

Because every long goodbye, no matter how painful, carries a hidden invitation: to live the rest of your days wide awake.

The Rest Stop

The Rest Stop

Stop.

Yes, you read that right.

Just like on long journeys, you need a rest stop otherwise you carry on and get exhausted and take your eye off the road. I don't want you to just drift along, I want you in the driving seat, alert and motivated.

I don't want you rushing straight on to the next chapter. You've just gone deep — really deep. You've time-travelled through your life, stitched together your quilt of memories, and faced some truths that most people keep buried. That's not light reading. That's not something to skim and tick off like a to-do list.

This is the halfway point of the BASTARD Method, and it's where I ask you to pause.

Here's why: real change doesn't happen in a mad dash. It happens in the spaces in between. In the week where you sit with what you've uncovered. In the moments where you notice the patterns in real life, not just on the page.

So, I want you to do something that might feel uncomfortable: put this book down. Right now. For at least a week.

Give yourself time to breathe. Notice what comes up for you. Notice the little shifts — what feels heavier, what feels lighter, what suddenly makes more sense.

If you're hesitating, if you feel like you "should" keep reading, ask yourself this:

What's the point of learning a new way of living if you don't give yourself the space to live it?

This is your line in the sand moment. You've done the prep work. You've laid out your quilt. You've faced your past and given yourself a reset. Now you get to step over that line and move forward differently.

So, close the book. Put it on a shelf, a desk, a bedside table. Wherever. And come back in a week.

When you do, we'll get into the next stage: aligning with your truth — building the foundations for the life you want, not the life you've been told to live.

See you in a week. I'll still be here.

Seriously, I wasn't joking when I said put the book down.

Chapter Eight

A is for Align

Align with your Truth

You've flicked the switch. You've proven you can move. Now we're going to make sure you're moving in the right direction — yours.

Because here's the thing: momentum without alignment is just running faster toward the wrong damn thing. And if you've spent years living by someone else's rules, chasing someone else's definition of success, or ticking boxes you never agreed to, you already know how that feels.

When you align with your truth, everything changes. You stop bending yourself into shapes that don't fit. You stop saying yes to things that drain you. You stop apologising for wanting what you want.

But first, you have to know what that truth actually is.

Quick Reality Check

- Do you even have goals right now, or are you just going through the motions?
- If you do have goals, are they really yours, or were they handed to you?
- Are your daily choices taking you closer to a life you want to live, or keeping you stuck in a life you've outgrown?
- Do the people you spend time with energise you, or leave you running on empty?

If some of those answers make you wince or if you're realising you've never stopped to ask yourself any of them, good. That's where we start.

The Conversation That Changed the Way I See Truth

Months after my hypnotherapist helped me realise it wasn't the spiders making me unhappy it was the life I was living, I met up with an ex-co-worker for one of our no-holds-barred, talk-about-anything catch-ups.

We met in a quiet pub, one of those places with sticky tables and warm lighting, where the pints came cheap, but the conversations always ran deep. We'd always been able to skip the small talk. That day, he pushed me to think about what life I truly wished I had.

He was happily married, had almost-adult children, a good job, hobbies he enjoyed, and a solid circle of friends. By most peoples "should" standards, he was winning at life.

And he was — or so it seemed.

Then he said something I'll never forget:

"Every now and then I think, if the doctor told me I had months to live, do you know what I'd do? I'd leave the wife, say goodbye to the kids, and I'd go work somewhere far away — building huts for families in need or helping communities who don't know the luxuries we take for granted. And I wouldn't even look back. The family have had the rest of my life. If I knew it was ending, I'd do what I WANT. No one else."

He didn't say it dramatically. No grand gesture. Just matter of fact, with a sip of his pint, like he'd been carrying the thought for years. And it landed in my chest like a stone. My breath caught. I realised the man who looked like he had it all was quietly living with the same ache I knew too well — the ache of being out of alignment with your truth.

What does this teach us?

That even people who look like they're "winning" by all the usual measures can still be living out of alignment with what they truly want.

It shows us that:

The "perfect life" can still be a cage if it's built on other people's expectations.

Truth often hides under loyalty, obligation, and habit.

Mortality cuts through the bullshit. When you imagine the clock running out, you stop thinking about what you "should" do and focus entirely on what you want to do.

Here's the real kicker: if you'd change everything the moment the clock started ticking, then you're already overdue for a change.

Why wait until you're given an end date to live the life you actually want?

Rules of Engagement

Alignment isn't just about what you love. It's also about what you won't tolerate.

For example: I will always help people. But I won't be treated like I should drop everything the second someone demands it. That's not kindness, that's being taken advantage of.

Being kind is not a weakness. But confusing kindness with compliance? That's where you lose yourself.

Ask yourself:

- What will I always show up for?
- What will I no longer tolerate?
- Where have I confused kindness with self-abandonment?

Write your answers. These are your rules of engagement. They don't just protect your time; they protect your energy — and energy is everything.

Permission to Care Differently

Somewhere along the way, many of us got sold the story that being a "good person" means being endlessly available. Say yes. Smile. Help. Don't rock the boat. Keep everyone comfortable, even if it means slowly disappearing yourself.

That story is exhausting — and it's wrong.

People-pleasing isn't kindness; it's a coping mechanism. It's what we learned to do to stay safe, accepted, or loved. It worked once. But now it costs too much.

Alignment asks you to unlearn that.
It asks you to stop proving you're good by burning yourself out for everyone else.
It asks you to care with purpose instead of obligation.

You still care deeply — that won't change. But you get to choose *where* your care goes.
You get to decide who earns access to your time, energy, and heart.

This isn't about becoming cold. It's about becoming clear.
It's the moment you realise that self-respect is not the opposite of kindness — it's the foundation of it.

So from here on:

- Care about what lights you up.

- Care about the people who meet you halfway.

- Care about your peace, your progress, and your joy.

It's not about not caring — it's about finally caring in the right direction. Caring about yourself as well as others, and caring in a way that everyone who deserves to benefit from your, does. And let the rest fall away without apology.

That's alignment.

Show Up Energy

Think about the roles you play in life: partner, parent, friend, colleague, leader, neighbour.

Ask yourself two questions for each one:

- How do I want to show up in this role?

- How do I want to be treated in this role?

Because people treat you the way you train them to. If you want respect, model it and demand it. If you want love, practice it and expect it. Alignment isn't just about living your truth — it's about shaping the way others interact with you too.

***

Exercises for Align with your Truth

1.Core Values Lock-In (Anchors)

A friend once told me that your values are like anchors: when you know what they are, you stop drifting. That idea stuck with me.

Sit down and ask yourself: *what really matters to me*? Write down whatever comes — family, freedom, creativity, peace, health, honesty, adventure. Then look for the themes.

Pick your five that matter most. Define what they mean to you (not a dictionary definition, but your definition).

Now ask: *am I living by these, or ignoring them*? When you honour them, life feels lighter. When you don't, resentment builds.

Your values are your compass. They stop you running in circles and point you towards choices that actually feel like yours. And when the bastards show up because they will those values are what keep you from being dragged off course.

And here's the kicker: don't just write them down and forget them. Use them. Check every big decision against them. If you just "go with the flow," don't be surprised if you wash up somewhere you never meant to be.

2.The 48-Hour Dare

Here's something that might rattle you. In the next 48 hours, pick one thing you know isn't aligned with you. A plan, a habit, a commitment, a relationship. Cancel it. Step away. Change it.

I once had a client who admitted that she dreaded going to a family members for coffee every week because it was just a bunch of women moaning and being negative about everything. She took the dare, and bravely cancelled the weekly commitment. She said the relief hit instantly, like she could breathe again.

What's yours?

Alignment Myths (And Why They're Crap)

Alignment is selfish. **No** — when you're aligned, everyone benefits because you're not bitter or half-alive.

Alignment means blowing up your whole life. **No** — sometimes it's one tiny adjustment that makes the shift.

Alignment makes life easy. **No** — life is still messy. But at least the mess is yours by choice.

Alignment is a one-time fix. **No** — it's ongoing recalibration. Like adjusting the steering wheel while you drive.

WARNING – Don't be the leak in someone else's life. If we are out of alignment then we can often become the pessimist or negative voice in other people's lives. Be aware of your words and the energy you put out before you look for fault in others.

3.The Reset Ritual

This is the line in the sand moment.

Grab a blank page. Draw a line down the middle. On the left, write the truths, habits, and roles that belong to "old me." On the right, write the ones that belong to "new me."

Then place that page on the floor. Stand up. Step over it. Literally.

It might sound silly, but trust me, the act of stepping across is powerful. A before and after. A reset.

When you do it, pause. Take a breath. Out loud, say something like: "I release the old me. I claim the new me." Or whatever words feel right to you in the moment. Don't just think it — speak it. Anchor it in your body. Make it feel real.

For me, one of those reset moments came the day I signed the lease on my dream apartment after leaving my relationship. On paper, it was just a contract and a set of keys. But when I opened that door, I felt peace. There were no noises in the walls, no dark corners hiding truths, no infestations. There was a spider's web on the door, but this time I didn't flinch — I didn't care.

Only looking back now do I realise what that meant. The things that once consumed my mind felt different because I finally had peace in my soul. That was my reset ritual, and I knew I had stepped into the life of "new me."

Some people light a candle before. Some rip the paper after. Some keep it as a reminder. There's no right way. The only rule? **Mark the moment.** Because this is the moment.

Alignment in Action

Alignment doesn't mean every day is perfect. It means every day feels like it belongs to you.

When you're aligned:

- You say yes without resentment and no without guilt.
- You wake up knowing you're moving in the right direction — even if it's slow.
- You're proud of the way you're living now, not just the life you're aiming for later.

The reward isn't just peace. It's energy. It's focus. It's momentum that comes from knowing you're building YOUR LIFE not anyone else's.

You've done the deep work. You've flicked the switch. And now, you've defined the foundation you're going to build on.

From here, every step you take is going to be rooted in who you are, not who you've been told to be.

Take a breath.

You've just reclaimed the part of you that knows what matters.

Now the work is protecting it — keeping your energy, boundaries, and peace aligned with that truth.

Because once you've remembered who you are, the next step is making sure the world around you remembers it too.

It's time to **rewrite the rules.**

***

"Good things come to those who wait."

Nope. Good things come to those who move. Waiting is just another form of stuck.

Rebel Reset: Proud to Be a Failure

Failure is just evidence you were brave enough to try. I've learned to wear my so-called failures like a badge, because they're the moments that forced me to realign with what I actually want.

Here's the thing about failure: it's rarely the end of the story. More often, it's a badly written first draft.

I once chatted with a taxi driver who told me about his daughter. She'd been bullied at school — not just once, but repeatedly. He told her to fight back. When she did, she got suspended. The parents had complained, the school ignored it, and when she defended herself again, they treated her like the problem.

He fought with the school but eventually pulled her out. To them, she was "failing." A kid with "anger issues." A parent who couldn't get it right.

But then she joined a new school. This one listened. A few weeks in, he got a call and braced himself for bad news. But it wasn't. The teacher wanted to praise his daughter. She'd taken children who spoke little English under her wing, helped them learn, and in return, they'd been teaching her Gujarati. She was excelling, shining, thriving. The school said she was the kind of student teachers dream of. They even created extra language classes for her.

Same child. Same parent. Different environment.

That first school thought they were dealing with a failure. The second school recognised they were looking at a star.

And here's what that taught me: sometimes "failure" isn't about you at all. It's about the environment. Or the rules you were forced to play by.

For me, this showed up in a different way. I spent years being a people-pleaser saying yes when I wanted to say no, agreeing to paths that didn't fit, choosing futures because they were expected of me, not because they were mine. And when those choices didn't work out? I called it failure.

But the truth? I wasn't failing at my life. I was failing at someone else's version of it.

There's no shame in realising you got carried away on a train that wasn't yours. But here's the thing: if you're going to stumble, stumble on your own path. If you're going to fall, let it be because you were brave enough to leap towards something you actually wanted not because you stayed quiet on a track that never fit you in the first place.

Because failing on your own terms isn't really failing at all. It's progress. It's proof. It's failing forward.

Fail forward into clarity.

Fail forward into courage.

Fail forward into the life that is actually yours.

And every time you fail forward, you're not going back to square one — you're moving one square closer to the life that's actually yours.

Chapter Nine

R is for Rewrite

Rewrite the Rules

You've done the work to remember who you are. Now it's time to protect her.

Because here's the thing: once you've started living by your own truth, the world doesn't always applaud. It pushes back. It tests you. And that's when you discover that alignment isn't a feeling — it's a practice.

So, I've said it before and I'll say it again: **the bastards are real.** They've been in my life, and I know they've been in yours. The ones who questioned your choices, tested your patience, drained your energy, or made you believe you had to shrink to be loved.

They can be people, habits, places, old versions of you — anything that tries to dictate your story for you.

This chapter is where you take the pen back.

The Question That Stopped Me in My Tracks

After I'd blown my world apart and ended my long-term relationship (yes, it took months of therapy before I finally made that life-changing decision), I went into a local coffee shop where the owners knew both me and my ex. One of the women looked at me and asked a question that, even now, makes me feel as stopped in my tracks as I did that day.

"Do you know what makes you happy?"

I laughed and said, "Yes, of course I do."

She didn't break eye contact.

"No, I mean really. You've spent ten years doing everything for him. Think about it. Do you know what happiness is by your definition not his and not you as a couple, just you?"

That question followed me for weeks. Every time I did something, I asked myself: *Do I even like this?*

Turns out, I did not like watching the reality TV shows we used to watch together. I stopped. I haven't watched one since.

I realised I liked walking more than cycling. I gave my bike away.

Even down to groceries I was still buying things I didn't even enjoy eating, just because I always had. It's like living on auto-pilot and never questioning why.

I was living in my dream apartment, and I thought that meant I was "happy." But changing my life was more than changing my address.

I needed to relearn who I was or should I say, who I wanted to become.

What I liked. What I disliked.

What brought me joy, peace, and love — **IN.**

What bored me, drained me, or pulled me back into my old life — **OUT.**

That even came down to friendships and boundaries. Some people had to go.

Simple? Yes.

Easy? Not at all.

But it was necessary — to lay the foundations for the life I wanted and make sure I didn't slip back into living someone else's version of it. I will ALWAYS say this, change is often quite simple but simple does not equal easy!

The Happy List (Reframed)

I remember deciding to spend a week noticing whether the things I did actually made me happy and if they didn't, to ask why I was still doing them. That week changed everything.

It sounds simple, but it pulled the rug from under all my autopilot habits. Every TV show, every meal, every walk, every conversation — I asked: *Do I actually like this?*

The answers were surprising. Some "yeses" reminded me of the spark I'd been missing. The "nos" showed me how much of my life was filled with things that weren't mine at all.

Try it. Just for a week. Pay attention to your yeses and your nos. Write them down if you want or just keep them in your head. By the end, you'll start to see a pattern — your pattern.

And if you're ever unsure, here's the tiebreaker: ask yourself, *"Is this old me or new me?"*

Because sometimes you do like the thing. But is it you **now**, or just a shadow of who you used to be?

Trust me when I say this works, I have seen it work for others I have coached and it is so simple to do and very eye (and heart) opening.

Rule of thumb: Setting boundaries is self-care.

Protecting Your Energy

If you discovered someone had secretly wired their electricity supply to your meter, you'd fix it immediately.
So why let people, habits, or environments siphon your personal power?

Think of your energy as currency. You wouldn't hand your wages to strangers in the street, so don't hand your energy to people or problems that keep you stuck.

Protecting your energy isn't about building walls; it's about having filters. Clear rules. A simple, *this is what I allow and this is what I don't* clarity that keeps your power invested where it matters.

If it costs you your peace, it's too expensive.

Below are the four types of personal energy — and how to start guarding them.

1. Physical Energy

Drains: Overcommitting, ignoring body cues, glorifying exhaustion.
Protectors: Rest before burnout. Eat real food. Honour movement and sleep.
Rewrite: *I will no longer treat depletion as dedication.*

2. Mental Energy

Drains: Overthinking, comparison, constant input.
Protectors: Create quiet. Choose fewer opinions. Stop trying to earn worth through productivity.
Rewrite: *My focus is my filter.*

3. Emotional Energy

Drains: Carrying other people's chaos, saying yes while your gut screams no.
Protectors: Practise emotional triage — if it's not yours to fix, let it go.
Rewrite: *Kindness without boundaries is self-betrayal.*

4. Spiritual Energy

Drains: Living out of alignment with your truth.
Protectors: Anchor with daily rituals — writing, walking, prayer, dancing, silence.
Rewrite: *Protect your light like it pays your bills.*

When Boundaries Get Tested

Here's the truth: even the strongest rules wobble when emotions, guilt, or old habits show up.

That doesn't mean you've failed — it means you're human.

Before life tests you, plan your response. Write it down, practise it, and keep it somewhere you can see until it becomes second nature.

If ___ happens, then I will ___ and say "___."

If a family member calls right as I'm winding down for the night, I'll send a message instead: "I'm heading offline now — I'll call you tomorrow when I can give you my full attention."

If a friend circles back to the same drama, I'll say: "I love you, but I can't hold this tonight. Let's talk when you're ready for solutions."

If someone invites me to something I don't have energy for, I'll say: "Thank you for thinking of me — I'm keeping my weekend clear for rest, but let's catch up soon."

Your calm, repeatable sentence is your lifeline when you're tired, triggered, or tempted to fall back into old patterns.

And if you slip? Repair it with honesty:

"I over-committed earlier — that doesn't work for me, so I'm stepping back."

No guilt. No essays. Just course correction.

Boundaries aren't about control — they're about clarity. They're how you love yourself out loud.

Self-Contracting: The Promise to Yourself

In *Align*, you met your values — what integrity means to you, what lights you up, and what drags you down.

Now it's time to move from *understanding* who you are to *committing* to it.

Think of this as drawing up a sacred agreement with yourself — a promise about what you'll continue to value and what you'll no longer tolerate.

Write it down. Date it. Sign it.

It doesn't have to be formal; it just has to be *true.*

Your contract might include boundaries around time, relationships, work, and — most importantly — **your energy.**

I will value...

I will no longer tolerate...

I commit to protecting my energy by...

Sign it. Date it. Keep it somewhere you'll see it every day.

This is you becoming the keeper of your own peace.

The 30-Day Clause

Every contract needs a review date. In thirty days, revisit your self-contract. Some rules will still fit; others will feel too small.

That isn't failure — it's growth.

Sign again. Refine. Keep rewriting.

Own It or Lose It

If you don't own your truth, someone else will write it for you and their version won't fit.

Stop waiting for permission. Stop waiting for perfect timing.

This is your life.

Protect it. Honour it. Rewrite it — on your terms.

Want to Go Deeper?

If this chapter struck a chord, there's a full **Boundary Playbook** waiting for you — a short, practical course that shows you how to communicate, enforce, and maintain boundaries in real life, without guilt or apology.

You'll find it inside the **Chapter Deep Dives: Rewrite the Rule** experience at https://thebastardmethod.com/.

Because once you've remembered who you are, the next step is learning how to stay that way.

***

"Don't get too big for your boots."

Fine. I'll get bigger boots.

"Don't air your dirty laundry in public."

Guess what — pretending everything's fine is what nearly broke me. Airing the truth is how I breathe now.

Truth Bomb: PIVOT

If you've never watched Friends, you'll miss the reference. But if you have, you probably already know the scene I mean.

Ross is trying to move a sofa up a narrow stairwell with Rachel and Chandler. The stairwell is too tight, the angles don't work, and chaos quickly takes over. He keeps yelling one word as the sofa gets stuck and wedged in increasingly ridiculous positions: pivot!

The more he says it, the less it helps — and the funnier it gets. The sofa never actually makes it upstairs, but the moment lives on as one of the show's most iconic.

Why am I telling you this? Because life often feels the same. You push and push, convinced you can muscle through, but the angle is wrong. The more you try, the more stuck you get. That's when it's time to do what Ross was trying to say all along: pivot.

Pivot means change direction. Try a new angle. Shift your weight, your perspective, your approach. If that doesn't work? Pivot again.

There's no shame in it. In fact, pivoting is often the smartest move you can make. Because eventually, you'll find the angle that works.

Chapter Ten

D is for Decide

Decide your own ending

You've done the work. You've cracked illusions, dropped the masks, silenced the critic, time-travelled through your past, aligned with your truth, and rewritten the rules.

Now comes the part no book, no coach, no mentor can do for you.

You decide how this ends.

This is your story. And like any great story, the final chapter is a choice. Two pathways. Two endings. Both lead to freedom. The question is: **which one feels like yours?**

So why two endings, you might ask?

Because this isn't about following my map anymore; it's about trusting your own.

Depending on where you are or who you're becoming you might choose differently each time you return to these pages.

Ending 1

If you tend to lean towards the spiritual, law of attraction, or "woo woo" ways, then stepping into your new self with an unclouded vision of the life you want can be all the motivation you need. Embracing your dream life and knowing who that person is, how they live, and how they feel is the perfect way to close this book.

So, if you're drawn to vision, energy, and the language of possibility, step into **Chapter 10A – Dream It, Feel It, Live It.**

Ending 2

And, if you just read that and thought "Nope, too fluffy," and you're more of a getting-shit-done kind of mindset, then unapologetic action-taking might be what lights you up.

so, if you're craving grounded momentum and action, jump to **Chapter 10B – Decide Who the F*** You Are.**

Either way, you're moving.

Go ahead.

Chapter 10a - Dream it, Feel it, Live it!

This is the pathway for the dreamers, the believers, and the ones who know in their bones that energy matters.

Here's the thing: your dream life won't just land on your lap. but when you set your intention, anchor your energy, and train your focus, life has a funny way of meeting you halfway.

This chapter is about turning everything you've worked on into a vision you can feel so deeply, it becomes inevitable.

Your Vision Board (Future in Pictures)

As I believer in the concept of the Law of Attraction, I have over the years embraced the art of manifestation to bring your thoughts into reality and have had some great successes. Not just the finding a parking space kind but the dream home, the partner, the job and money and so much more. So, I know it works, but here is the part of the process that people tend to ignore, you can set your intention but if you don't do the work, if you don't live in alignment and make decisions that lead you on the path to the thing you want to attract, then it doesn't just happen. If you embrace the magic, then join me as we walk through vision boards.

I've created vision boards for years. Some were scrappy cut-outs from magazines. Some were images downloaded boards. One time, I even doodled mine on post it notes stuck to my fridge.

Here's why it works: your brain loves pictures. When you see an image that excites you, it anchors a feeling. And when you repeat that feeling often enough, you start making choices that move you towards it without even realising.

So, grab a board (physical or digital) and fill it with images that represent what you want to bring into your life — the apartment, the travel, the freedom, the joy, the laughter, the career, the love. Don't filter yourself. Dream big.

Every time you look at it, take a second to breathe it in and say to yourself: "That's mine. I'm moving towards it already."

Put your board up somewhere you can see it every day, take a photo and save it as your phone screensaver. Keep it central in your life so that it acts a bit like your values and compass. Am I making this decision as my future dream life? Will it help me get what I want to manifest?

Affirmations (Your Daily Script)

Forget cheesy slogans. An affirmation is just a statement of truth you repeat until your brain believes it.

Write a handful that feel powerful to you, like:

I am building a life that excites me.

I trust myself to make bold choices.

I am worthy of joy, love, and peace.

Say them to the mirror. Write them in your journal. Stick them on your phone screen. You're not brainwashing yourself — you're reprogramming your inner script.

The Dream Day Journal

Here's a game-changer: once a week, write out your "dream day" as if it already happened.

Start with: "Today was a great day. I woke up feeling..." and go from there. Describe where you were, who you were with, what you did, how you felt.

Let it flow. Don't hold back. This is your safe space to imagine the version of your life you're moving toward.

And here's the magic: when you read it back, your body doesn't know the difference between "imagined" and "real." It just knows it felt good. That good feeling fuels you to take steps that make it real.

The Pause-and-Feel Ritual

Dreaming isn't about staring at a board and wishing. It's about feeling it.

Every day, even if it's just for sixty seconds, pause. Close your eyes. Picture your dream life. See it in as much detail as you can. Then — feel it. The joy. The freedom. The peace. The excitement.

That feeling is the frequency that keeps you aligned when the world gets noisy.

Dream it. Feel it. Live it.

Repeat.

Chapter 10b – Decide Who the F*** You Are!

Here's the truth: nobody's coming to rescue you. You have to step up and rescue yourself.

This is the unapologetic ending. No fluff. No manifesting unless that's your jam. This is about drawing the line, slamming the pen down on the old story, and deciding who the f*** you are from this moment on.

If Dream It was about vision, Decide It is about velocity. It's about not waiting for permission, not waiting for the stars to align, not waiting for one more sign that you're "ready." You're ready when you decide you're ready.

And deciding means action.

The Starter-for-Ten Plan

When I say, "ten moves," I don't mean ten overwhelming projects that will take you a year to tick off. I mean ten bold statements of intent. Ten things that prove to you that you've decided.

Think of it like throwing down markers in the ground — your flags that say: this is me now and mean it!

Here's how you build it:

1. **Pick one bold "f*** yes" move.** Something that feels scary but thrilling. Maybe it's signing up for that course. Maybe it's sending the message you've been avoiding. Maybe it's applying for the job you keep telling yourself you're not ready for.

2. **Pick one "no more" move.** One thing you're done tolerating. Cancel it. Quit it. Say no to it. Walk away. That alone shifts your energy like nothing else.

3. **Pick one self-celebration.** Not a reward for later. Now. Do something that feels like you're honouring yourself. Buy the flowers. Take the day off. Toast yourself for making it this far.

4. **Pick one boundary move.** Decide one rule that protects your peace. Write it down. Say it out loud.

Put it into action the next time someone crosses it.

5. **Pick one connection move.** Reach out to someone who lifts you up. Or go find new people who match the energy you're stepping into.

6. **Pick one health move.** Your body is your fuel. Choose something that feels like care, not punishment. A walk, a stretch, a proper night's sleep.

7. **Pick one money move.** Look at your finances and make one decision that future-you will thank you for. Save, invest, budget, or stop spending on crap that doesn't serve you.

8. **Pick one creativity move.** Do something that lights you up just for the joy of it. Paint, write, cook, sing — whatever makes you feel alive.

9. **Pick one courage move.** The thing you've been putting off because it terrifies you. Do it anyway. Even if your voice shakes. Especially if your voice shakes.

10. **Pick one alignment move.** Something small that makes your daily life look more like the truth

you've been uncovering in this book. Swap one old habit for one new one.

Here's the thing: these don't have to be "perfect." They just have to be done.

Because every time you cross one off, you're not just moving forward — you're proving to yourself that you are a person who decides. Proof that you are no longer living on auto-pilot.

And ten decisions? That's momentum. That's proof. That's you rewriting the whole damn story.

My Starter-for-Ten (No Judgement Please!)

So, what kind of coach would I be if I didn't show you how I used this tool myself?

Did I do all ten in one day? Absolutely not. But over the months, as I worked through what my new normal looked like, I ticked them off one by one. Here goes:

1. Took the apartment. For context, I used to walk past that block and say, "one day I'll live there." So, when I ended my relationship and needed a fresh start, I made the bold move. Rent was more than double my old place, but I decided I'd make it work. And I did. That apartment gave me peace.

2. Released old connections. Some people tied to my old life would have judged me for moving there. I signed the lease and, in my mind, released them too. No drama. No fallouts. Just outgrowing.

3. Went to my first meditation class. Local village hall, up in the loft. A little bizarre. But the new me was hungry for peace, so I said yes.

4. Protected my new space. For six months, I only gave my address to a select few. And anyone who entered got the rule: "Leave your drama at the door. Positive vibes only."

5. Made new friends. People who matched the energy of where I was heading, not where I'd been.

6. Started walking round the reservoir. One lap before work each day. Fresh air. Movement. Space to breathe again.

7. Cut the debt. I left the relationship with debt. Took out a loan, cut up the credit cards, and swore off them. Seven years on, still no credit cards. Best financial decision I ever made.

8. Reignited creativity. Started creative writing. At first, just for me. Then, unexpectedly, it turned into a side career as an author.

9. (Left intentionally blank at the time). Not because I failed, but because I left space for what was coming. Sometimes, the most powerful move is to leave yourself open.

10. (Still evolving). Because life doesn't stop at ten. Once you start deciding, you don't stop.

This list wasn't about perfection. It was about proof. Proof that I wasn't just talking about change — I was living it.

Now It's Your Turn

Make your Starter-for-Ten. Don't overthink it. Don't try to get it "right." Just get it down.

Ten decisions. Ten markers. Ten bold declarations of the life you are choosing from this point forward.

Because if you don't decide, someone else will.

And their script won't come close to the one you'd write for yourself.

So go on. Decide who the f*** you are.

And then, for the love of your future self — **prove it.**

Part Three – Moving Forward

You've done the work. Now it's about carrying it with you, through daily practices, through declarations, and through the reminder that the real you has always been enough.

Chapter Eleven

If Journaling is your thing

Journaling is a well-documented, research-backed technique, and I've mentioned it throughout this book but honestly? It's not my go-to. I'm more likely to rant in the notes app on my phone or scribble something on the back of an envelope than to sit down with a pretty notebook.

But I know for many of you, journaling is your safe space. Pen to paper. Thoughts to words. Chaos to clarity.

So, if journaling is your thing, this chapter is your bonus gift; a way to take everything you've uncovered in these pages and weave it into your daily life.

Why Journal?

Because the real work isn't just reading a book. It's catching yourself in the everyday moments when you're about to slip back into old patterns and giving yourself a reset in real time. Journaling is one of the simplest, most powerful ways to do that.

It's not about writing a novel, being neat, or having the perfect bullet journal spread. It's about showing up to the page as you; raw, real, messy, honest.

Think of it as your private conversation with the most important person in your life: YOU.

The Morning Practice:

Set the Tone

Mornings are fresh starts. A chance to decide who you want to be before the day decides for you.

Here are some prompts to kick off your day:

My day today will be...

(Write it in the present tense, as if it's already happening.)

What I want to feel by the end of today is...

One thing I choose to do for me today is...

This is not a to-do list. It's a declaration list. Even if life throws curveballs, starting your day by claiming your intention shifts everything.

The Evening Practice:

Reflect and Reset

Evenings are your reset button. A chance to look back without judgement, extract the lessons, and let go before tomorrow begins.

Prompts to close your day:

My day today was...

(Again, write it in the present tense, like telling a friend about it.)

What worked out for me as I wrote this morning was...

What didn't go the way I wanted — and why?

If I faced the same situation again, I would...

(Example: "Instead of eating the doughnut, I'd order the coffee.")

This isn't about beating yourself up. It's about noticing. Awareness is the crack in the mirror where change begins.

Layer in Declarations

You've learned by now that affirmations are nice, but declarations are power. They're not wishful thinking — they're ownership.

So, here's how to finish your journaling each day:

Write or whisper one declaration that anchors you back into the work you've done.

Here are some examples to start you off:

"I am more than enough."

"I choose to live by my own expectations, not anyone else's shoulds."

"The real me has always been enough."

Sample Morning Journal Entry

Date: Tuesday

My day today will be...

Today will be calm and productive. I'll keep my head clear, get through my work without overthinking, and leave space for myself.

What I want to feel by the end of today is...

Proud that I kept my boundaries. Lighter in my body. Less distracted.

One thing I choose to do for me today is...

Go for a walk at lunch instead of scrolling on my phone.

Declaration:

I choose to live by my own expectations, not anyone else's "shoulds."

Sample Evening Journal Entry

Date: Tuesday

My day today was...

Messy but good. I got most of my work done and had one proper laugh with a colleague that shifted my mood.

What worked out for me as I wrote this morning was...

I actually took the lunchtime walk. Fresh air really did clear my head, and I felt less sluggish in the afternoon.

What didn't go the way I wanted — and why?

I ate the doughnut at 4pm. Honestly? I was tired and bored. It wasn't hunger, it was habit.

If I faced the same situation again, I would...

Make a coffee instead. Or go back outside for five minutes.

Declaration:

The real me has always been enough.

Make It Yours

If journaling feels like a chore, keep it short. Two minutes in the morning, two in the evening.

If you love it, expand. Write pages. Add doodles. Stick in photos. Swear. Make lists. Whatever makes it feel alive for you.

This isn't about doing it right. It's about making it yours.

And remember: these words aren't just ink on paper. They're reminders. Reset buttons. Anchors for the real you you've been uncovering through this journey.

When in doubt, write it down. And if writing isn't your thing, talk it out, record it on your phone, or scream it into the wind. The medium doesn't matter. The act of noticing, declaring, and choosing again does.

***

If you love journaling and really want to take this deeper, I created something specifically for you! The Rebel Reset Card Deck, 31 cards with different journal prompts to help you to push deeper, one journaling nudge at a time, link will be available on https://thebastardmethod.com/cards.

Chapter Twelve

Conclusion: Handing Over the Baton

You made it.

You've walked through illusions, masks, critics, memories, truths, and rules. You've dared to dream or decided who the f*** you are. And now, the baton is officially in your hands.

This book was never about me — it's always been about you. About the life you're ready to claim, the choices only you can make, and the person you're brave enough to become.

Because here's the truth: no book, no coach, no friend, no partner can do this for you. They can cheer you on, guide you, inspire you — but the action? The ownership? The transformation? That's all on you.

And I know you can do it. Because you've made it this far.

The 100 Success Tokens

I want to leave you with one final tool. Something simple, but ridiculously powerful.

Draw out or print 100 little tokens (circles, squares, stars — whatever feels good). Number them 1 to 100. Pin them somewhere you'll see every single day — your fridge, your mirror, your office wall, or inside your journal.

Here's how it works: every time you achieve something — big or small — fill one in.

Said no when previously would have just complied? Token.

Had that difficult conversation? Token.

Took the first step toward the dream you wrote about? Token.

Protected your peace on social media? Token.

Stopped tolerating what drained you? Token.

Some tokens will be huge milestones. Some will be tiny moments no one else notices. Both counts.

Because what you're really tracking isn't just achievements — it's proof. Proof that you're not stuck. Proof that you're capable of change. Proof that you're building momentum one choice at a time.

And when you hit 100? Celebrate. Decide now how you'll mark it.

A weekend away? A day off just for you? A bottle of champagne? A tattoo? A mirror selfie with the biggest grin you've ever worn.

Whatever it is, make it yours.

And to give you no excuses, there are ten pages of tokens in the toolkit section at the back of this book.

Final Word

The B.A.S.T.A.R.D Method™ was never meant to fix you. You were never broken.

What it gives you is something different: a reset, a rebellion, a reminder that you get to decide.

Decide what you believe.

Decide what you'll tolerate.

Decide what you want.

Decide how you'll live.

Because if you don't — someone else will.

So, here's my closing dare to you: don't let this book be something you just read and put on a shelf. Let it be the spark. The line in the sand. The point where you decided.

And when you look back, months or years from now, may you smile at all the tokens, all the bold moves, and all the moments where you stopped waiting for permission and started living.

This is your baton now. Take it. Run with it. Make it yours.

Epilogue – The Real You is Enough

Epilogue – The Real You is Enough

Back in 2019, when I was still a struggling life coach, I hadn't found my identity yet.

I'd survived a relationship break-up. I'd built my dream home.

On the outside, it looked like I was piecing life back together.

Inside, I was searching. Searching for purpose. Searching for myself.

I came across an empowerment event for women entrepreneurs and thought, go for it.

I walked into the room, sat at a table full of strangers, and immediately felt like a fraud.

The women around me were established, polished, talking the talk of how wonderful they were and how they were smashing it in their businesses.

I smiled. I nodded. But deep down, I felt small.

The next speaker came on stage. She didn't strut or shout. She simply spoke — calm, honest, captivating.

And then she paused. She asked us all to stand up and close our eyes.

And then she said the five words that changed my life:

"The real you is enough."

She said it again.

"The real you is enough."

And again.

"The real you is enough."

And again.

"The real you is enough."

And one more time, firmer now, like she was planting it in our bones:

"The real you is enough."

The fifth time... something cracked open inside me.

I was struggling to breathe. A single tear broke free, slowly making its journey down my cheek. Then another.

I cried. Quietly. Reserved. Trying not to embarrass myself.

But as I sat back down and looked around the room, I realised I wasn't the only one.

Had we never heard those words before?

I couldn't tell you much more about the event after that moment because that was the moment everything changed.

"I am enough" had never resonated with me. It always felt surface level. A phrase people parroted while still holding up their masks.

But that day, I understood.

It's not about being "enough" in the version you show the world.

It's whether the real you, behind the mask, behind the mirror, behind the performance can believe it.

That's why her words hit harder:

The REAL me is enough.

The overweight me.

The struggling-to-keep-it-all-together me.

The grieving daughter me.

The daughter pretending her mum didn't have dementia me.

The partner who carried someone else's illness for years.

The messy, imperfect, unpolished me.

Later that day, when she walked past me, I had to reach out. I had to tell her how her words moved me.

And she hugged me.

In that hug, I broke down with ugly tears. And she just held me.

No mask. No performance. Just me — allowed to exist as I was.

I don't think she ever realised the impact she had.

And I've waited until the very end of this book to tell you this story because I want you to know it and hear it loudly:

THE REAL YOU IS ENOUGH.

THE REAL YOU IS ENOUGH.

THE REAL YOU IS ENOUGH.

THE REAL YOU IS ENOUGH.

THE REAL YOU IS ENOUGH.

And in these pages, I've tried to hold space for you too, so you can drop your mask, you can breathe again, remember what it feels like to simply be.

Sometimes you feel lost but you were never truly lost, it was just a feeling.

Sometimes you feel broken but you are not broken. None of us are.

We feel broken because society judges us, because we measure ourselves against impossible expectations.

Some of those expectations we set for ourselves.

Some were set for us.

It's time to take back the narrative.

When you feel lost, when you feel broken, that's your signal to pause.

To breathe.

To reset and pivot as many times as you need until you feel like you again.

That might be a new you. Or it might just be the old you with a few tweaks.

And guess what? You get to decide. Decide who the real you will be from this day forward.

Carry this with you. Write it. Say it out loud. Whisper it when you forget. Shout it when you remember.

Let it become the truth you live by every single day:

"The real me has always been enough."

Now it's over to you.

Love,

Sarah x

Your Declaration

This is my pledge to myself.

To speak it. To write it. To live it.

Today I declare:

I have broken the illusions that kept me small.

I choose to care for myself first, without guilt.

I silence the critic that never belonged to me.

I honour the child within and carry her forward with love.

I live by my truth, not by anyone else's "shoulds."

I rewrite the rules of my life to serve me.

I decide, every day, who the f*** I am.

And above all: The real me has always been enough.

Signed: ______________________________

Date: ________________________________

(Keep this declaration close. Say it each morning. Write it each evening. Whisper it when you forget. Shout it when you remember.)

Acknowledgements

To the people who created the moments that changed me:

Thank you. Some inspired me, some challenged me, some broke me open in ways I didn't understand at the time. But all of you helped me to believe.

To my brothers; Anthony & Stevie:

Thank you for walking beside me through the hardest chapters of our lives. Losing Mum and Dad changed us forever but facing that loss together gave me strength I could never have found alone.

To my auntie Christine:

Who was there for my mum and I through our darkest times. Best friends for life. Every day I want to ACHIEVE just for you! Keep smiling and never forget our laughter too!

To my partner, Lee:

Who has shown me what true love and happiness can really feel like. Here's to our continuing on this adventure we call life together!

To my friends, Sunita, Angeline, Niasha, Nguyet, Kay, Kal and Thomas:

You stood beside me through the messy chapters of life — thank you for your patience, your encouragement, and your love.

To my ex, who loved me the only way he knew how.

You changed my life, I will never forget our hugs and happy times, not even "a little bit"! Remember, I will always be your biggest supporter. Don't let your bastards grind you down.

To the people who shared their stories with me, and to the women I've had the privilege of coaching:

Your courage and honesty gave me the conviction to write this book. You reminded me that healing is never linear, but always possible.

To the mentors, therapists, and speakers who crossed my path:

Sometimes for a moment, sometimes for a season — thank you for the wisdom, the perspective, and even the jolts I didn't know I needed.

And finally — to the bastards.

The ones who doubted me, dismissed me, broke my heart, or made me question my worth. You became the sparks that lit this fire. Without you, there would be no B.A.S.T.A.R.D Method™, and this book wouldn't exist.

And to you, the reader — thank you for saying yes to yourself. The fact that you're here, holding these pages, tells me you're ready for something more. That is the bravest thank-you of all.

The B.A.S.T.A.R.D Method™ Toolkit

So here we are. You've reached the end of the book. I've finished being your guide through the method — but before you go, I want to leave you with something practical.

Because here's the truth: you can read all the words, nod along, feel the spark, but the genuine change only happens when you do the work. When you take the ideas off the page and weave them into your actual life.

That's what this toolkit is for.

Inside these pages you'll find every exercise we touched on in the book, gathered together in one place so you don't have to flick back and forth. Think of this as your workbook, your reset button, your place to scribble, doodle, and get messy with your own breakthroughs.

A couple of things to remember:

This is not homework. You don't have to do every single exercise. Choose the ones that click with you. The ones that make you pause and think, "Oof, that one's got my name on it."

Change doesn't come from perfect notes. It comes from imperfect action. Write in half sentences. Cross things out. Draw a stick figure if that's all you've got. It still counts.

Come back to it often. These tools aren't one-and-done. They're for recalibrating whenever life pulls you off track.

So, grab a pen.

Breathe.

And dive in.

Because your future? It's waiting for you to build it, one bold scribble at a time.

Chapter 4–Break the Illusion

In Chapter 4, you started breaking down the stories that were never yours to carry. Here are the tools we explored to help you spot illusions and loosen their grip:

- The Spider Test-a quick gut-check to see if what you're feeling is real danger or just fear in disguise.

- The Should Audit–a place to log all those "shoulds" you've been carrying and decide which ones you're finally dropping.

- The Rebellion Room–if you want to go deeper, this is where you imagine the mental clutter you've been hoarding and start clearing it out. Whilst there is no visual, I have added some guidance for completeness.

The Spider Test

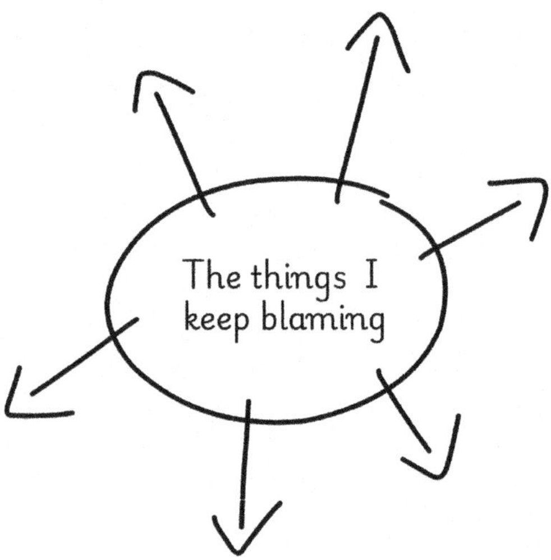

Instructions:

Write down the "spider" in your life — the thing you keep blaming.

Around it, write the bigger truths it might be hiding.

Example:

Spider = "My job is killing me."

Truths hiding underneath = I'm in the wrong career. I've been ignoring burnout. I don't feel valued.

The Should Audit

The Shoulds I've collected	versus	What is true for me

Instructions:

Fill the first column with every "should" you're carrying.

In the second, rewrite it with your truth.

Example:

I should be married by now → I want a relationship that excites me, not a timeline.

I should be further in my career → I'm learning at my pace.

The Rebellion Room

This is your private space. Nobody else can enter. Nobody else will ever see inside. In here, you get to smash the illusions that have held you hostage.

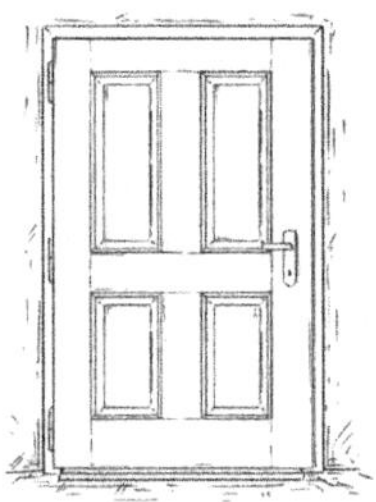

Step 1–Fill the Room

Imagine your Rebellion Room lined with mirrors. Each mirror shows an illusion you've been carrying:

The "shoulds" that kept you small.

The roles that drained you.

The lies you told yourself just to get through the day.

Write or doodle those illusions on this page.

Step 2–Smash Them

When you're ready, take a pen and *smash* them. Scribble, cross them out, crack the mirrors on the page. Tear it if you want to.

Step 3–Lock the Door

Close it up. Those broken illusions stay in the Rebellion Room. You don't take them back with you.

Step 4–The Truth You Carried Out

Complete the sentence below, making notes here if you want.

"When I walked out of the Rebellion Room, I carried this truth with me...

Chapter 5-Adjust Your Mask

In Chapter 5, we looked at the masks you wear — the performance, the smile, the "I'm fine" act — and how they suffocate you if you never take them off. These exercises are about giving yourself permission to breathe again:

- Permission to Breathe – a simple, repeatable pause where you stop, inhale, exhale, and remind yourself you matter too.
- The Selfish Hour – your guilt-free space to rest, recharge, or do something that's just for you.
- The Oxygen Leak Audit – track where your energy is being drained so you can plug the holes.

***

Permission to Breathe

Instructions: Take micro-pauses in your day.

Start with 15 seconds of breathing.

Build up to 30.

Then to a full minute.

The Selfish Hour

How would I spend an hour that's just for me, with zero guilt? Write it in the thought bubble so you don't forget!

The Oxygen Leak Audit

Instructions:

For a week, track where your time and energy go. At the end of the week, circle one drain you'll plug.

Energises me:

Drains me:

Neutral:

Chapter 6-Slay the Inner Critic

In Chapter 6, we met the villain in your story: that voice in your head that tells you you're not enough. These tools are designed to put it in its place:

- Cast your villain – Giving it a name removes it from your voice.
- The Bastards Greatest Hits – Match their top five criticisms with a comeback.
- Fact or Fiction – Find evidence first before you believe it.

Your critic is the villain. Time to stop letting it run the script.

Cast your Villain

Imagine your critic as a villain in your story.

Give it:

- A name
- A face
- A voice

The pettier or more over-the-top, the better, that way its easier to separate it from your own voice.

Write or sketch about it in the space below:

The Bastards Greatest Hits

Write down the top 5 lines your critic always throws at you.

- For each one, write a comeback in your strongest, most unapologetic voice.

Example:

Critic: "You're not good enough."

- You: "Good enough for who? And why the hell do I care?"

Critic Greatest Hits
VS
My Comeback

Fact or Fiction

Next time the critic speaks, pause and run it through this filter:

1. Is this a proven fact with evidence?
2. Or is it an assumption, prediction, or old story?

If it's fiction, rewrite it into a fact you'd like to be true.

Example:

Critic: "You'll embarrass yourself."

Rewrite: "I might feel nervous, but I'm capable and prepared."

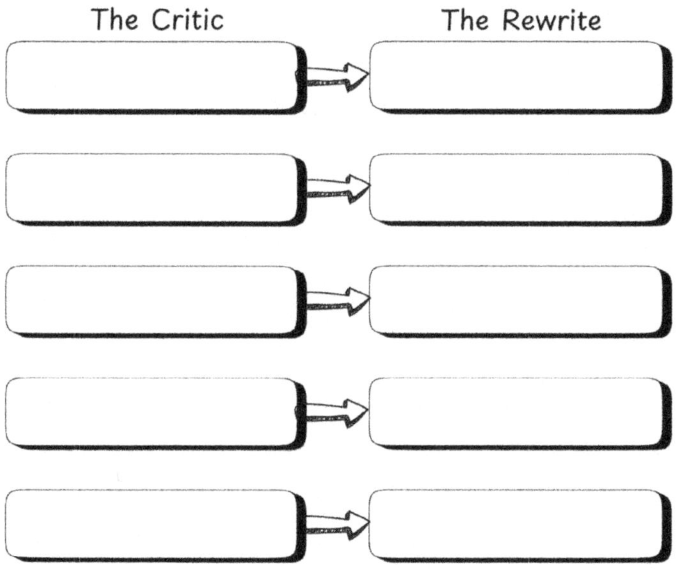

Chapter 7-Talk to Your Time Traveller

Your past shaped you, but it doesn't define you.

- The Memory Quilt

Draw a quilt (grid of squares). On one side, fill with happy memories. On the other, with painful ones.

- Three-for-Three Shift

Pick your 3 hardest memories. For each:

Recall the sadness for 15 seconds.

Then recall a happiest memory for 45 seconds.

Repeat to anchor positive over painful.

- The Blanket of Love

Visualise wrapping yourself in a quilt made only of loving, warm memories. Write down how it feels. Keep that image for when you struggle.

***

The Memory Quilt

Instructions:

Fill the happy side with small sketches, words, or photos that spark warmth and joy. On the reverse, capture difficult memories that shaped you.

Three for Three Shift

Instructions: Pick 3 of your hardest memories and note them in the storm clouds. Then pick 3 of the happy memories and pop them in the sunshine. Bit cliché but it is simple and no one needs overcomplicated right now.

For each one, take 15 seconds to recall the pain then, anchor it by spending 45 seconds reliving a happy memory instead.

Wrap Yourself in the Blanket and Feel the Love!

In tough moments, picture the blanket wrapping around you with each of the happy memories touching your skin. What feelings does it hold for you?"

The Rest Stop

At this point, I asked you to put the book down for a week. Here's the worksheet that marks that reset.

A blank space to write, doodle, or capture anything that came up for you in the pause.

Chapter 8-Align with Your Truth

In Chapter 8, you found your anchors. The parts of you that stop you drifting into someone else's story. These tools help you hold that alignment:

- Rules of Engagement – define what you'll always show up for and what you'll never tolerate again.

- Core Values Lock-In – identify your 5–7 non-negotiable values and see where you're honouring or ignoring them.

- The 48-Hour Dare – one bold, immediate action to step into alignment now.

***

Rules of Engagement

Instructions: Fill in both boxes to define your rules for how you'll engage with the world.

I will always...

I will no longer tolerate...

Core Values Lock-in

Write out your values that mean the most to you that you can anchor yourself to.

Prompts to help:

When have you felt most fulfilled?

When have you felt most resentful?

Which values feel exciting now that weren't important before?

My Top 5 Core Values

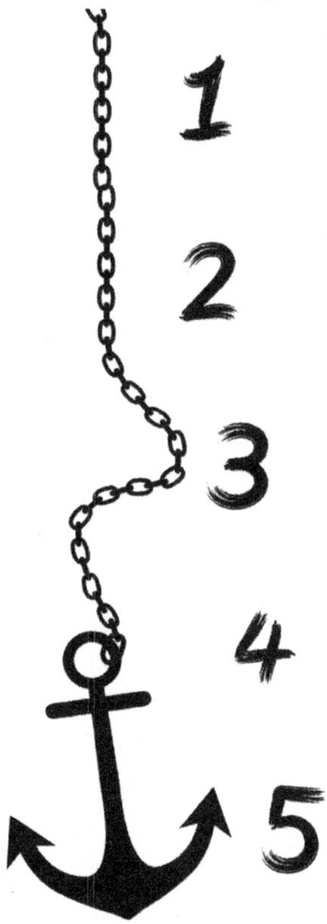

48 Hour Dare

Think the popular quote "he who dares, wins." Embrace this for 48 hours, pick one thing out of alignment in your life.

Cancel it, change it, or let it go within 48 hours.

Chapter 9-Rewrite the Rules

In Chapter 9, you stopped playing by rules that were never yours and wrote your own. These tools pull it all together:

- Stop, Start, Continue – return to this tool and choose the rules you'll stop following, the ones you'll start, and the ones worth keeping.

- Social Media Detox – Take time to consider what you want to see and don't see across your social media feeds to protect your peace.

- Energy Protection: Guarding Your Rules – define your "peace is priceless" rules and commit them to your diary, your phone, even your wallpaper.

***

Stop, Start, Continue

Instructions:

Revisit your earlier notes.

Now layer in the rules you've just rewritten.

Decide which behaviours or boundaries belong in each category.

Stop

Start

Continue

Social Media Detox

Who do I need to unfollow, mute, or block to protect my peace?

What do I want to see more of in my feed?

Example:

I unfollowed any news platforms and newspapers and celebrity news because it was always repetitive, catastrophising and depressing. I blocked friends who shared nothing but drama.

I followed inspirational quote pages, people who inspired me and other coaches but not the spammy kind.

Energy Protection

On the left: People / Places / Habits That Drain Me. On the right: "People / Places / Habits That Fuel Me."

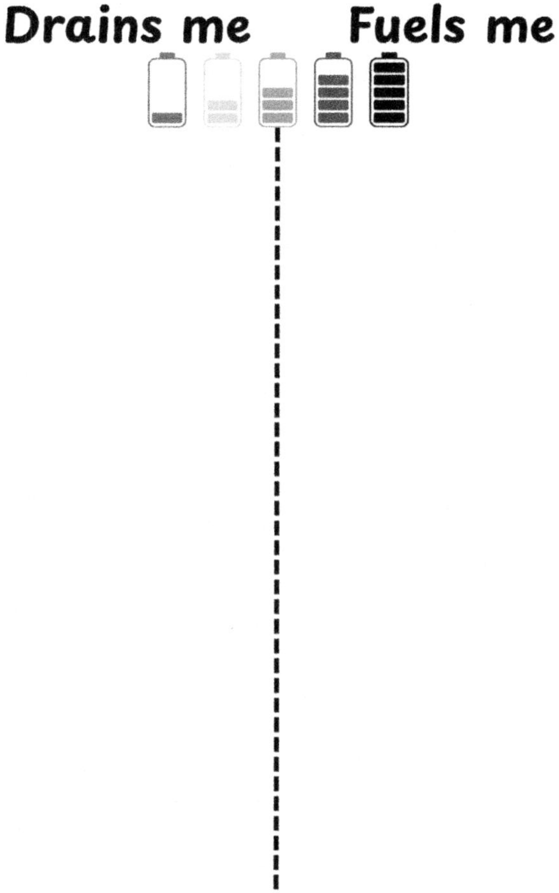

Chapter 10-Decide your own ending

The final chapter gave you two different ending options, this is to ensure you are consciously making the decision to rebuild and how.

Here you will find:

- Dream it – Build your vision board, this one can just be some notes until you decide to do your own.
- Dream Day Journal – An example page but you can use your own notebook.
- Affirmation builder – Helps you to find your own words of strength.
- Decide it – Starter for Ten

***

Dream it Vision Board

Dream Day Journal

Instructions:

Write as if you're journaling at the end of a dream day, living your future life now.

Today was perfect because

Affirmation Builder

Write 3 affirmations that align with your dream life. Example: "I am building a life that excites me."

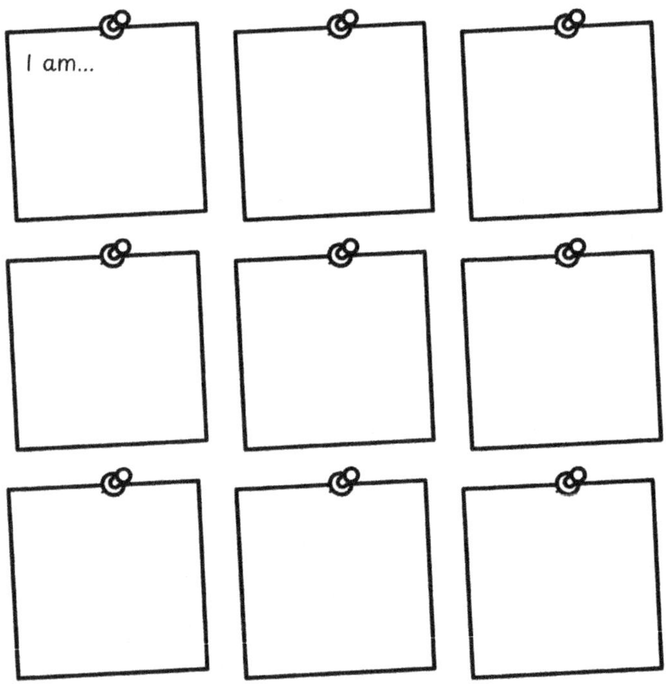

Decide It-Starter for Ten

1.
2.
3.
4.
5.
6.
7.
8.
9.
10.

100 Success Tokens

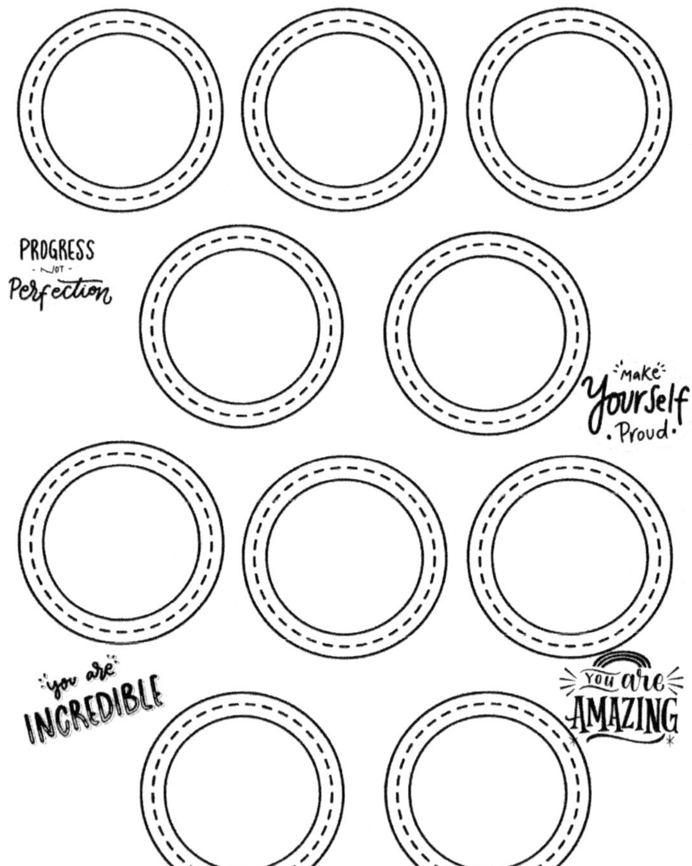

Good Vibes
only
PUSH
yourself
TO BE
GREAT
BE
Fearless

Stop Wishing Start Doing
make it happen
Things Change Inside You
stay STRONG

PROGRESS NOT Perfection
Make Yourself Proud
you are INCREDIBLE
You are AMAZING

Stop Wishing Start Doing
You Can Do THIS
Build your own Future
Keep GOING

STOP Wishing START Doing
make IT happen
THINGS Change INSIDE YOU
stay STRONG

Good Vibes
only
PUSH
yourself
TO BE
GREAT
BE
Fearless

Stop Wishing Start Doing
You Can Do This
Build your own Future
Keep Going

STOP
Wishing
START
Doing
make
IT
happen
THINGS
Change
INSIDE YOU
stay
STRONG

Good Vibes only
PUSH yourself TO BE GREAT
BE Fearless

One Last Word

You've done the work. You've broken the illusions, dropped the masks, silenced the critic, time-travelled your memories, aligned with your truth, and rewritten the rules. Now you've got one hundred spaces waiting to celebrate your wins — your proof that this isn't just theory, it's action.

Every token you tick is a reminder: you're building the life that belongs to you, not the one you were told to settle for.

This isn't the end. It's the beginning of everything that comes next.

So don't let this sit on a shelf. Live it. Tick it. Own it.

Because the bastards don't get the last word — you do.

And if you reach a step where the pages aren't quite enough, remember: you don't have to walk this path alone. The B.A.S.T.A.R.D. Method™ continues beyond these pages — through the deck, the course, and coaching support — for when you're ready to go deeper.

Start here: **TheBastardMethod.com/**

Final Final Word

For my readers who stuck with this to end, you can find a page on my site that only you and I know exists – Check out https://thebastardmethod.com/reader-secret

About the author

Sarah Shard is a writer, coach, and creator of *The B.A.S.T .A.R.D. Method™* — a rebellious self-healing framework for women who are done holding it all together.

After navigating grief, burnout, and the slow unravelling of a life that looked fine on the outside but felt broken underneath, Sarah rebuilt herself from the ground up. She turned her own breakdown into a breakthrough and now helps other women do the same — guiding them to rewrite their stories, reclaim their energy, and rebuild their lives on their own terms.

When she's not supporting others, coaching, or writing, Sarah can usually be found walking by the water, dancing in her kitchen, or hunting for good coffee and quiet corners. She also writes fiction — short stories and cosy village novels where everything happens for a reason.

She lives in Yorkshire, England, where the hills and wild weather remind her that transformation is never tidy but it's always worth it.

Visit **www.thebastardmethod.com** to explore her tools, courses, and community.

Printed in Dunstable, United Kingdom

72774406R00143